Power, Threat, or Military Capabilities

US Balancing in the Later Cold War, 1970–1982

Carmel Davis

UNIVERSITY PRESS OF AMERICA®, INC.
Lanham • Boulder • New York • Toronto • Plymouth, UK

Copyright © 2011 by
University Press of America,® Inc.
4501 Forbes Boulevard
Suite 200
Lanham, Maryland 20706
UPA Acquisitions Department (301) 459-3366

Estover Road
Plymouth PL6 7PY
United Kingdom

All rights reserved
Printed in the United States of America
British Library Cataloging in Publication Information Available

Library of Congress Control Number: 2011931309
ISBN: 978-0-7618-5551-4 (paperback : alk. paper)
eISBN: 978-0-7618-5552-1

∞™ The paper used in this publication meets the minimum
requirements of American National Standard for Information
Sciences—Permanence of Paper for Printed Library Materials,
ANSI Z39.48-1992

Contents

Acknowledgments		v
1	Explanations of Balancing: Power, Threat, and Military Capabilities	1
2	Balance of Power: Population, Military Personnel, and Economic Resources	17
3	Balance of Power: National Security Expenditures and the Military Burdens	31
4	Balance of Threat: US Assessments of Soviet Intentions	51
5	Balance of Military Capabilities: Sufficiency of General Purpose Forces	84
6	Balance of Military Capabilities: US Wartime Prospects	98
7	Conclusions	108
Bibliography		115
Index		121

Acknowledgments

I would like to express my appreciation to Avery Goldstein, G. John Ikenberry, and William C. Wohlforth for their advice. I would like to express particular appreciation to Stephen Biddle. I would like to express appreciation to Richard Betts, Edward Mansfield, and Marc Trachtenberg for comments and to Stephen O'Connell and Herbert Klein for comments and advice about economics.

Finally, I would like to express appreciation to Martin Meyerson and James Spady for their early encouragement.

Chapter One

Explanations of Balancing: Power, Threat, and Military Capabilities

US balancing against the Soviet Union varied in intensity over the course of the Cold War. The last intensification began when the Soviet Union intervened in Afghanistan in late 1979. The Cold War ended when Soviet domination of Eastern Europe collapsed less than ten years later, and the Soviet Union itself was tossed into the "dustbin of history" in 1991. In retrospect, the Soviet Union appears to have been weaker than the US. Why did US balancing against the Soviet Union intensify in the early 1980s?

US behavior is potentially explained by two mainstays of international relations theorizing, balance of power and balance of threat. Both hold that countries exist in anarchy in which there is no superordinate authority to protect them so each must provide for its own security. They do so by balancing. A country may balance internally by generating military forces to defend itself, or, more broadly, to dissuade by imposing high costs. In addition or instead, it may balance externally by forming or strengthening alliances with other countries it believes will cooperate in defense or dissuasion.

Balance of power and balance of threat differ in their explanations of what causes balancing. According to balance of power, countries balance against power, which is comprised of material resources like economic size, military expenditures, and number of military personnel. Expanding balance of power's argument, countries with more resources are more powerful; countries with less balance by generating more resources either internally or by adding the resources of other countries by forming alliances. Balance of threat claims to refine and improve upon balance of power.[1] It argues that a country balances because another country or coalition appears especially dangerous because it has power, offensive capability, geographic proximity, and aggressive intentions. Balance of threat allows a powerful country to balance against a weaker country and so to become stronger, something contrary to balance of power.

Balance of power and balance of threat provide competing explanations of US behavior. According to balance of power, US balancing intensified because it perceived that the Soviet Union was increasingly powerful in terms of material resources. According to balance of threat, the powerful US balanced because it perceived that the weaker Soviet Union was threatening.

There are gaps in the logic of balance of power. First, there is a gap between the variable, power, and the military capabilities that are its causal mechanism and its effect. Balance of power argues that countries are fearful of being conquered or compelled and preserve their sovereignty by balancing, building capabilities and forming alliances able to defend and dissuade. The ability to conquer and compel, or to defend and dissuade, is about military capabilities. Balance of power uses material resources, either generated internally or additively by alliance formation, as a proxy for military capabilities. However, they are not a reliable proxy.[2] If they were, more powerful countries, defined as countries with more material resources, should regularly prevail in war. But, after the mid-nineteenth century, they do not.[3] For example, Arab countries should have repeatedly prevailed against Israel, and Japan should have been repeatedly defeated in its wars with China and Russia. Material resources are inputs to military capabilities, not the capabilities themselves. The gap between power and military capabilities may reduce the ability of balance of power to explain international relations. Exploration of this gap justifies case studies that test balance of power.

Second, there is a gap between power and its component parts. Balance of power treats power as a single, undifferentiated variable. That single variable is comprised of a variety of elements, like population, military expenditures, and economic size. However, balance of power does not specify how the elements compose power and thus how to compare different endowments or how much change in which component elicits balancing. The situation is still more opaque when countries balance externally: how should the endowments of countries be aggregated? The incomparability of different kinds of material resources and the absence of an explanation about how they compose power makes balance of power hard to operationalize reliably.

Third, comparisons of quantities like economic size and military expenditures, central elements of power, are difficult. Even after conceptual problems like what parts of a military program should be measured and how to do it are resolved, the process encounters the problem that comparison of the prices of one country in terms of the prices of another will tend to overstate the value of the first. For example, US estimates of Soviet military expenditures in terms of dollars tended to overstate Soviet expenditures. The effect is always to worsen the apparent relative power position of the country whose currency unit is used to make the comparison. This issue, the index number problem, is discussed in chapter 2.

Finally, to the extent that balance of power focuses on military forces, which it at times calls capability, it asserts that countries with larger forces are more powerful than those with smaller forces. This is problematic in two ways. First, it does not distinguish between the ability to attack and to defend. However, large forces configured for defense may have poor prospects of success attacking small forces and small forces configured for offense may have good prospects against large ones.[4] Second, it ignores how a country deploys its forces. For example, a less powerful country might concentrate its forces and successfully attack a more powerful country. Germany concentrated its forces when it overran France, Belgium, and the Netherlands in 1940.

Balance of threat partially fills the gap between material resources and military capabilities by its employment of offensive power, the ability to conquer and compel, as a cause of balancing, although it is cautious about its significance. However, balance of threat does not consider "defensive power," the ability to defend against or dissuade another country's offensive power. In the absence of explicit consideration of "defensive power," balance of threat remains reliant on proxies for balancing behavior.

There are also gaps in the logic of balance of threat. First, balance of threat emphasizes aggressive intentions, saying they are "key." However, aggressive intentions are not well defined and can be subjective. If the threshold for perception of "aggressive intentions" is low, balance of threat becomes impossible to falsify. Second, it is not clear how the elements of aggregate power, geographic proximity, offensive power, and (perception of) aggressive intentions compose threat. How much of each is needed, and what is the proportion that produces a threat sufficient to drive balancing behavior? Finally, measurement of power, a component of threat, is as difficult in balance of threat as it is in balance of power.

Balance of military capabilities fills these gaps by arguing that countries balance against the ability of others to conquer or compel them. Offensive military capabilities are what may enable one country to conquer another and, by threat of conquest or imposition of intolerable costs, to compel another. Generation and maintenance of sufficient military capability to defend with good prospects of success against conquest, or, more broadly, to dissuade by imposing high costs, constitutes balancing behavior. The result is an equilibrium between a country's ability to defend and dissuade and the ability of others to attack.

Balance of military capabilities answers the anomaly for balance of power of powerful countries balancing against weak ones by arguing that countries balance against offensive military capabilities rather than material resources. According to balance of military capabilities, the US balanced in the early 1980s because it was not confident about its ability to defend vital territory and interests from Soviet attack whether or not it believed the Soviet Union was powerful or had aggressive intentions.

Balance of military capabilities is related to balance of power and balance of threat, but it is significantly different. It differs from balance of power by focusing on the output of military capability rather than the input of resources and distinguishing the ability to attack from the ability to defend. Where balance of power gives substantial weight to economic capabilities, balance of military capabilities focuses on military ones. It is related to balance of threat's argument that the offense-defense balance is a cause of balancing. However, balance of military capabilities considers the ability to defend and explicitly assesses both sides of the offense-defense balance. Where balance of threat is cautious about the significance of offensive power, balance of military capabilities argues that the offense-defense balance is what causes balancing. Where balance of threat emphasizes aggressive intentions, balance of military capabilities emphasizes the abilities of countries to act.

Balance of military capabilities provides a more leveraged explanation of balancing behavior. Balance of threat uses aggregate power, geographic proximity, offensive power, and aggressive intentions to explain why powerful countries at times balance against weaker ones where balance of military capabilities uses the offense-defense balance alone. Moreover, it is more leveraged than balance of power. Instead of the economic and military resources used by balance of power, balance of military capabilities argues that countries balance against what other countries can *do* with their military capabilities.[5]

The purpose of this book is threefold. The first is historical: it explains a major case, US balancing against the Soviet Union in the late Cold War. These three theories serve as interpretive frameworks that focus the search for evidence in the documentary record. The second and third are theoretical: it proposes balance of military capabilities that fills gaps in the logics of balance of power and balance of threat, and it tests these three theories using the documentary evidence. This test is important for three reasons. First, balance of power and balance of threat are central theories but there are few head-to-head tests of them. Which better explains this case? Which is fortified and which is infirmed? Second, offense-defense theory is generally considered as a cause of war rather than a cause of balancing. Balance of threat argues that offense-defense theory can help explain balancing but includes it with aggressive intentions and geographic proximity. Balance of military capabilities emphasizes the offense-defense balance as the primary cause of balancing. I test it against the aggressive intentions significant in balance of threat and the material resources important to balance of power. Third, balance of military capabilities provides a competing explanation of the anomaly of balancing by powerful countries against weaker ones. A major component of balance of threat's answer is that they balance against aggressive intentions. However, intentions are hard to measure objectively and require capability to fulfill. Balance of military capabilities argues that strong countries balance against countries that are weaker in terms of material resources but have sufficient military capability to attack successfully the vital interests of the strong country. It answers why the US, for example, balances against "rogue states" without reference to aggressive intentions. Balance of military capabilities may provide an answer to a puzzle for balance of power with greater parsimony than balance of threat using a much less subjective methodology than assessment of intentions. Finally, balance of military capabilities has policy implications. Balance of power expects balancing against the US. Balance of threat does not because potential balancers do not perceive that the US has aggressive intentions. Balance of military capabilities argues that others will balance against the US if the US possesses military capabilities that allows it to conquer or compel them and won't if it does not. Balance of military capabilities expects balancing by China against the US in the form of maritime and air capabilities. It does not expect balancing by Germany or Japan, as balance of power theorists projected in the 1990s, because the US does not possess the capability to conquer or compel either.[6]

So what? On one level, not much. Like balance of power, balance of military capabilities focuses on material resources and can readily be substituted into balance of power arguments. Offensive realism already emphasizes military elements of power. Balance of military capabilities could be seen as balance of threat focused on offensive power and deemphasizing aggressive intentions. On another level, a great deal. First, balance of power and balance of threat make divergent predictions about this case. Which, if either, is right? Second, balance of power and balance of threat have gaps in their logic. Balance of military capabilities fills those gaps. While the pieces of balance of military capabilities are present in balance of power and balance of threat, they have not been assembled in this way. Balance of military capabilities provides a more leveraged, direct explanation of balancing and provides policy-relevant insight into international relations. In doing so, it may provide a better explanation of an important historical episode and a better guide to future policy.

The next section considers the three theories of balancing in greater detail. The following section discusses theory testing, case selection, and the observable implications of the three theories.

THREE EXPLANATIONS OF BALANCING: POWER, THREAT, AND CAPABILITIES

Balance of Power

Though balance of power has a long history as an analytic framework, a significant problem with the concept is the absence of agreement about what is meant by the term. Claude wrote in 1962 that "If its meaning is not shrouded in mystery, it is at least cloaked in ambiguity."[7] Waltz wrote in 1979 that "If there is any distinctively political theory of international politics, balance-of-power theory is it. And yet one cannot find a statement of the theory that is generally accepted."[8] Wohlforth wrote in 1993 that Waltz's statement was still essentially true.[9] Jervis wrote in 1997 that "Balance of power is the best known, and perhaps the best, theory in international politics, although there is no agreement as to exactly what the theory holds, let alone whether it is valid."[10] Levy stated in 2002 that 'nearly all of the ambiguities in conceptualization and causal specification' he observed in 1989 "continue to plague the literature on the balance of power."[11]

Major issues underlying this absence of agreement include motivations for balancing and whether the focus is on balancing or the production of balances of power. Classical realists, exemplified by Morgenthau, Wolfers, Claude, and Gulick, focus on the role of human nature, especially a desire for power. They focus their analyses at the level of countries and emphasize deliberate balancing behavior by statesmen. The result of this balancing is an equilibrium of power. Morgenthau, for example, explicitly emphasizes the role of human nature and argues that "the aspiration for power on the part of several nations, each trying either to maintain or overthrow the status quo, leads of necessity to a situation that is called the balance of power and to policies that aim at preserving it."[12] For Morgenthau, balance of power means a situation "in which power is distributed among several nations with approximate equality." If one country tries to alter this situation, a second power will increase its own power so that it can resist and frustrate the first country's policy.[13] Wolfers argues that to defeat or render impossible any attempt to dominate them, "two or more powers could be counted upon to line up almost intuitively against any power that threatened to become their superior." The chief instruments of the balancing process are competition for allies and armaments. While the outcome might appear nearly automatic, the success of the balancing process depends upon the choices of statesmen.[14] Claude characterizes balance of power as a "system" with a number of "rules," distinguishes between automatic, semi-automatic, and manual balancing, and argues that the outcome will be a "reasonable stability of order with no more than moderate use of violent techniques."[15] Writing about Europe in the period of the Napoleonic wars and the Congress of Vienna, Gulick asserts that balance of power explanations assume a limited group of independent neighboring countries of relatively equal power. The primary aim of the balance of power was to insure the survival of independent countries. This entailed the preservation of the state system, something that was accomplished by preventing the preponderance of any one country by means of alliances. Alliances would be made for reasons of expediency and so might be short-lived.[16]

Neorealists, exemplified by the defensive realism of Waltz and the offensive realism of Mearsheimer, focus on the role of structure and the production of balances of power. Waltz argues that the existence of actors seeking survival in anarchy causes the recurrent formation of balances of power and so emphasizes the influence of the structure of international politics on the countries that compose it. According to Waltz, a "properly stated" balance of power theory assumes that countries are unitary actors who, at a minimum, seek their own preservation and, at a maximum, seek universal domination. They use internal and external means in "more or less sensible ways" to achieve their ends. The condition of its operation is that two or more countries operate in a self-help condition. The expected outcome is balances of power.[17] Waltz argues that 'balances of power tend to form whether some or all countries consciously aim to establish and maintain a balance,' that is without the intentions of statesmen and even if some countries do not engage in balancing behavior.[18] The offensive realism of Mearsheimer argues that countries look for opportunities to maximize their power so to maximize their odds of survival while thwarting others from gaining power at their expense by balancing. Countries balance by "seriously committing themselves to containing their dangerous opponent. In other words, they are willing to shoulder the burden of deterring, or fighting if need be, the aggressor."[19] Mearsheimer's countries behave like Morgenthau's, if not more aggressively, for Waltzian motives of security that can only be satisfied by regional hegemony.

Both classical realists and neorealists expect the production and maintenance of balances of power. They differ in motivations and whether countries always engage in balancing, with Waltz explicitly arguing that at times they may not. The issues of motivation and whether countries always balance are moot when there is a bipolar distribution of power, as in the Cold War, because both classical realists and neorealists share expectations about US behavior and so may be treated as a single balance of power explanation. Waltz argues that who is a danger to whom is never in doubt in the great power politics of a bipolar world. Each is 'intensely and constantly' concerned about changes in the military and economic capability of the other, there are no peripheries because each is concerned that the others gain will be its loss, and each is aware that it must look to itself for its own security.[20]

Power approaches generally define power in terms of material resources. For Morgenthau, the elements of national power include geography; natural resources, including food and raw materials; industrial capacity; military preparedness, including technology, leadership, and quantity and quality of armed forces; the distribution of population and demographic trends; national character and morale; and the quality of diplomacy and government.[21] For Waltz,

> The economic, military, and other capabilities of nations cannot be sectored and separately weighed. States are not placed in the top rank because they excel in one way or another. Their rank depends on how they score on all of the following items: size of population and territory, resource endowment, economic capability, military strength, political stability and competence.[22]

Mearsheimer distinguishes between latent and military power. "Latent power constitutes the societal resources a state has available to build military forces" and is measured in terms of wealth because it "incorporates both the economic and demographic dimensions of power."[23] Military power, however, is more important:

> ... the balance of power is largely synonymous with the balance of military power...The most powerful states...are those that possess the most formidable land forces. This privileging of military power notwithstanding, states care greatly about latent power, because abundant wealth and a large population are prerequisites for building formidable military forces.[24]

Arguing that land power is the dominant form of military power but that it is limited by large bodies of water, Mearsheimer measures military power by estimating the relative size and quality of opposing armies and then assessing air forces and the power projection capability of armies.[25]

Balance of Threat

Balance of threat claims to refine balance of power and to explain phenomena that balance of power cannot. As such, it claims to be a more powerful theory. It shares the assumptions that countries seek at least self-preservation and that they will do so by balancing behavior but it differs substantially in that it argues that power alone is insufficient to explain balancing behavior. Balance of threat theory is closely associated with Walt, who focuses on aggregate power, geographic proximity, offensive power, and aggressive intentions.[26] With respect to *aggregate power*, a country with more population, industrial and military capability, and technological sophistication poses a greater threat than one with less. Aggregate power is essentially the power employed by balance of power. With respect to *geographic proximity*, Walt argues that the ability of a country to project power declines with distance so nearby countries may pose a greater threat than those that are far away. Balance of threat argues that countries with *offensive power*, "the ability to threaten the sovereignty of or territorial integrity of another state at an acceptable cost," are more threatening than those without.[27] Offensive power "can result from superior numbers, more effective exploitation of existing capabilities, technological developments, political propaganda, and subversion."[28] It is closely linked with aggregate power, but it is a function of the offense-defense balance and the mix of forces each country acquires. Because offensive capability can take many forms, it is hard to measure and Walt is cautious about its significance.[29]

What decisively differentiates balance of threat from balance of power is *aggressive intentions*. Walt argues that "states that are viewed as aggressive are likely to provoke others to balance against them" and that "intention, not power, is crucial."[30] Walt illustrates aggressive intention with the examples of Nazi Germany, Qadhafi's Libya, and Wilhelmine Germany. Each of these countries had a high propensity to attempt to compel another. Such compellence might involve initiation of war or, because a country might initiate hostilities in response to attempted compellence by another, acceptance of risks that initiation of compellence might lead to war. Hitler remilitarized the Rhineland, assimilated Austria, and threatened war in order to dismember Czechoslovakia before initiating wars in an attempt to conquer Europe. He repeatedly disregarded the balance of power through 1941 because of his assessment of British and French resolve and Soviet resilience. Libya sent a submarine to sink the Queen Elizabeth II in 1973, provoked a war with Egypt in 1977, raided Tunisia in 1980, mined the Red Sea in 1984, and provided significant support to terrorist organizations at least up to the bombing of Pan Am 103 in 1988 and UTA 772 in 1989. Wilhelmine Germany repeatedly sought to compel other European powers, repeatedly ran risks that might lead to war, and, when war erupted in 1914, invaded Belgium and France.

Walt argues that the US and its allies had greater aggregate power than the Soviet Union and the Warsaw Pact and the Soviet Union devoted massive resources to building offensive forces. He also argues that the Soviet Union had aggressive intentions in the Cold War, citing their:

> ... counterproductive reliance on threats and intimidation, ranging from Stalin's pressure on Turkey, Iran, and Norway to the more recent attempts to browbeat NATO into halting deployment of intermediate-range nuclear missiles. The invasion of Afghanistan and the periodic interventions in Eastern Europe, Soviet support for terrorist organizations, and events such as the downing of a Korean airliner in 1983 also reinforce suspicions about Soviet intentions.

Finally, the Soviet leaders have never abandoned their public commitment to promoting world revolution.[31]

Offense-Defense Theory and Balance of Military Capabilities

Offense-defense theory distinguishes between the relative ease of offense and defense and argues that the offense-defense balance has significant effects on international politics. Jervis uses the offense-defense balance to explain the frequency of war and argues that the balance originates in technology and geography. Jervis characterizes offense as relatively easy when "it is easier to destroy the other's army and take its territory than it is to defend one's own. When the defense has the advantage, it is easier to protect and to hold than it is to move forward, destroy, and take."[32] Quester focuses on technology as a cause of the balance, and argues that offense dominance leads to higher frequency of war and larger states.[33] Van Evera argues that the balance originates in military factors like technology, doctrine, force posture and deployment; geography; regime popularity; and diplomatic factors like collective security systems, defensive alliances, and balancing. Offense dominance makes war more likely.[34]

Except for its role in balance of threat theory, where Walt is cautious about its significance, offense-defense theory is primarily a theory of war causation and frequency rather than an explanation of balancing behavior. Where balancing does enter consideration, it is secondary to war causation and frequency. For example, Van Evera includes balancing behavior by neutral states along with collective security systems and defensive alliances as diplomatic factors that help cause an advantage for the defense and so make war less likely.[35] However, this is a factor in an argument about war causation, not an argument about balancing even though it could be read in terms of balancing.

The focus of offense-defense theory, the ease of conquest, is also the focus of balancing explanations. Balancing explanations argue that countries fear conquest or domination and so engage in balancing behavior to make conquest or domination by others more difficult. However, where offense-defense theory addresses the cause of balancing, the ease or difficulty of conquest or compellence, both balance of power and balance of threat use proxies. Balance of power uses material resources and argues that countries balance because another country has more inputs that it might use to conquer or compel. Balance of threat uses threat, especially aggressive intentions but also aggregate power, offensive power, and geographic proximity. Both expect countries to balance by increasing their power, and both measure power in terms of material resource inputs generated either internally or externally by alliances.

Balance of military capabilities argues that military capability is the fundamental cause of balancing behavior. Offensive military capability is what may enable one country to conquer or compel another. Generation and maintenance of sufficient military power to dissuade constitutes balancing behavior. Dissuasion by defense may be accomplished by possession of adequate conventional forces. Dissuasion by deterrence may be accomplished by conventional forces sufficient to make conquest prohibitively expensive or by possession of nuclear weapons. Countries choose the level of military capability to generate by a net assessment of how well their forces could dissuade the offensive capability of others, both today and in the forecast future. If a country is not confident about its prospects in a war, it will increase it military capabilities.

Balance of military capabilities shares offensive realism's emphasis on the importance of military forces. However, balance of military capabilities differs in its approaches to assessment of forces. Offensive realism uses a side-by-side assessment, comparing the quantity and quality of forces and assesses the larger, qualitatively superior force as more powerful. Balance of military capabilities incorporates the offense-defense balance that observes that forces differ in their ability to attack and defend and emphasizes head-to-head assessment by analyzing wartime prospects. Where offensive realism measures forces by comparing the inputs of quantities and quality, balance of military capabilities assesses the output of what those forces can do.

Balance of military capabilities argues that the economic components of power are of derivative importance. A large, sophisticated economy can generate and maintain larger, more sophisticated forces than one that is smaller and less sophisticated. However, it takes time to translate economic capability into military capability so possession of a stock of adequate military capabilities is more important at any given time. In the context of a prolonged war, what matters is the ability of economic factors to produce a flow of sufficient military capabilities to continue operations as the initial stock and intermediate flows are consumed in operations.

It also argues that the geographic proximity is of derivative significance. Geography is important because the difficultly of projecting, operating, and sustaining military forces increases with distance. Balance of military capabilities argues that a country will balance against others that can conquer or compel it, whether nearby and so not faced with distance or far away and able to project capability over distance. In addition, it argues that countries dependent on trade and resources in geographically disparate areas have far-flung interests and must also be concerned with military prospects in each theater. Balance of military capabilities argues that countries balance against others able to project military capability into areas where they have vital interests.

Balance of military capabilities can explain why powerful countries balance against weaker ones. Powerful countries balance against less powerful countries that possess military capabilities able to threaten their territory and vital interests. They are not concerned about aggressive intentions *per se*, but about the ability to fulfill intentions. Those capabilities may be the product of intention, but intention alone is insufficient.

Balance of military capabilities can also explain why powerful countries ally with each other. Balance of threat says they do so because they do not perceive aggressive intentions among themselves but do perceive other, less powerful countries as threatening. For example, it can explain the NATO alliance between the US, Britain, and France, and it can explain the coalition between the US and China in the 1980s, all of whom were armed with nuclear weapons, by arguing that none harbored aggressive intentions toward the others when they were allies or members of a coalition. Balance of military capabilities argues that countries are concerned with their prospects in war. None of these countries harbored good prospects of success in a war with another member of its coalition so none believed it necessary to balance against the others. Each was worried about its prospects in a war with the Soviet Union so each saw the utility of an alliance or participation in a coalition.

CASE SELECTION AND THEORY TESTING

In addition to using the three theories to analyze an important case, this book tests the three theories. US balancing in the late Cold War is a good case for testing these theories. First, the test is about whether a theory explains balancing. This is the major case of balancing since the end of the intense balancing of the early Cold War. These theories should explain this case. The question is not about whether the independent variable of a theory, whether it be power, threat, or military capabilities, reliably produces balancing so it is not problematic to select a case on the dependent variable. Second, there is change in the value of the independent variable of each of the three theories over time so it is possible to observe the level of congruence between the independent variable of each theory and balancing behavior. In addition, this is a very strong test of balance of threat because data are sufficient to use process tracing to test whether the US perceived that the Soviet Union had aggressive intentions. If the US did, that should be abundantly present in the declassified record.

To test competing theories, each should have observable implications that can be verified or falsified by analyzing the case. If the implications of a theory are not borne out by the data, that theory is weakened. Observable implications should be unique so that evidence fortifies or weakens that particular theory. There are four unique observable implications of these three theories. The first is about the distribution of power. In the bipolar distribution of power of the Cold War, both classical realist and neorealist balance of power theories expect that the US was concerned about the level and change of Soviet power. If balance of power is correct, the Soviet Union should be increasingly more powerful than the US. Balance of power would also be fortified if the Warsaw Pact was increasingly more powerful than the West. Balance of power will be infirmed if the US was more powerful than the Soviet Union or if the West was more powerful than the Warsaw Pact. Chapters 2 and 3 assess the distribution of power.

The second is about aggressive intentions. A central element of balance of threat's explanation of US balancing is that the US perceived that the Soviet Union had aggressive intentions. If this is true, there will be substantial evidence in the assessments of the US intelligence community, the strategy studies and statements of the National Security Council (NSC), and the statements of the members of the NSC. Balance of threat will be infirmed if the US perceived that Soviet intentions were not particularly aggressive. Chapter 4 assesses whether the US perceived that the Soviet Union had aggressive intentions.

The third is about military capabilities. Balance of military capabilities explains US balancing by arguing that US military capabilities were increasingly insufficient to defend vital territory and interests against a Soviet attack. Balance of military capabilities will be strengthened if the US could have had lessening confidence in its ability to defend against a Soviet attack, and it will be weakened if the US could be confident. Chapter 5 assesses the offense-defense balance in terms of general purpose forces (conventional forces armed with nuclear weapons for use within a theater).

A second observable implication of balance of military capabilities is the perceptions of a country's leadership about its prospects in war. Balance of military capabilities expects that the US leadership was not confident that the US had good prospects in a war with the Soviet Union and generated military capability so that it would. Balance of military capabilities will be weakened if the US leadership was confident that the US had good prospects in a war with the Soviet Union. Chapter 6 considers how US leaders viewed US prospects in case of war with the Soviet Union.

What if more than one theory is fortified? For example, what if the US balanced because it was less powerful then the Soviet Union, the West was less powerful than the Warsaw Pact, the US perceived that the Soviet Union had aggressive intentions, and the US could not have reasonable confidence in its ability to defend its vital interests? Balance of military capabilities would claim that it fills gaps in the logics of balance of power and balance of threat, and that its variables are the actual cause and effect where the others use proxies. However, it is challenging older, established theories so they must have priority if they provide equally sound explanations. Of the two older theories, balance of threat is the challenger and so must yield to the established balance of power if their explanations are equally sound.

Thus, the sequence to evaluate these theories is to consider balance of power, then balance of threat, and then balance of military capabilities. Balance of power will be fortified if the US was weaker than the Soviet Union or if the West was weaker than the Warsaw Pact. If the US or the West was more powerful, balance of threat and balance of military capabilities have an opportunity to explain US balancing. Balance of threat will be fortified if the US perceived that the Soviet Union had aggressive intentions. It will be further fortified if balance of military capabilities is infirmed because US military capabilities were sufficient. Balance of military capabilities will have an opportunity if balance of threat is infirmed. It will be fortified if the US was more powerful than the Soviet Union or the West was more powerful than the Warsaw Pact, the US did not assess the Soviet Union as having aggressive intentions, and if US military capabilities were insufficient to defend vital territories and interests from a Soviet attack and the US leadership was not confident that the US had good prospects in a war with the Soviet Union.

NOTES

1. Stephen M. Walt, *The Origins of Alliances* (Ithaca: Cornell University Press, 1987), p 263 and "The Progressive Power of Realism," in *Realism and the Balancing of Power: A New Debate*, ed. John A. Vasquez and Colin Elman (Upper Saddle River, NJ: Prentice Hall, 2003), p. 62.

2. Stephen Biddle, *Military Power: Explaining Victory and Defeat in Modern Battle* (Princeton: Princeton University Press, 2004), pp. 191–196.

3. Ibid., pp. 20–23. Using data from the Correlates of War Project (COW), population correlates with victory in .59 of the seventy-nine cases between 1822 and 1990, all of the thirteen cases between 1822 and 1860, and .52 in the remaining cases. Military expenditures correlates with victory in .73 of 52 cases for which data are sufficient since 1822 and .68 of forty-five cases since 1860. Military expenditures is the hardest number to estimate with confidence, especially in near-real time. Military personnel correlates with victory in .58 of all cases, all of the first thirteen cases, and .52 of the remaining sixty-two cases for which data are sufficient. COW's Composite Indicator of National Capability correlates with victory in .59 of seventy-nine cases and .51 of the sixty-six cases after 1860. Data are from "National Material Capabilities (v3.01)" and "COW Inter-State War Data, 1816–1997 (v3.0)," www.correlatesofwar

.org. Importantly, COW warns "...the quality and quantity of the [national material capabilities] data vary greatly from state to state and from year to year."

4. Stephen Biddle, "Rebuilding the Foundations of Offense-Defense Theory," *Journal of Politics* 63, no. 3 (2001), p. 743 and Biddle, *Military Power*, pp. 192–193.

5. The assessment of the offense-defense balance and thus the operationalization of balance of military capabilities may be more complex than the assessment of the components of balance of power and balance of threat. However, assessment of the balance of power, as discussed in chapters 2 and 3, involves overcoming significant obstacles like index number effects, estimation of military expenditures, and counting rules for military equipment and personnel. Assessment of intentions can be extraordinarily difficult. More importantly, balance of military capabilities focuses attention on the variable most proximal to the effect, the ability to compel or conquer, dissuade or defend.

6. Kenneth N. Waltz, "The Emerging Structure of International Politics," *International Security* 18, no. 2 (Fall 1993).

7. Inis L. Claude, Jr., *Power and International Relations* (New York: Random House, 1962), p. 12.

8. Kenneth N. Waltz, *Theory of International Politics* (New York: McGraw-Hill, 1979), p. 117.

9. William Curti Wohlforth, *The Elusive Balance: Power and Perceptions During the Cold War* (Ithaca: Cornell University Press, 1993), p. 3.

10. Robert Jervis, *System Effects: Complexity in Political and Social Life* (Princeton: Princeton University Press, 1997), p. 131.

11. Jack S. Levy, "Balances and Balancing: Concepts, Propositions and Research Design," in *Realism*, ed. Vasquez and Elman, p. 128. See also Jack S. Levy, "What Do Great Powers Balance and When?" in *Balance of Power: Theory and Practice in the 21st Century*, ed. T.V. Paul, James J. Wirtz, and Michael Fortman (Stanford: Stanford University Press, 2004), p. 29.

12. Hans J. Morgenthau, *Politics Among Nations: The Struggle for Power and Peace*, 5th ed. (New York: Knopf, 1978), p. 4 and p. 173.

13. Ibid., p. 179.

14. Arnold Wolfers, "The Balance of Power in Theory and Practice," in *Discord and Collaboration: Essays on International Politics* (Baltimore: Johns Hopkins University Press, 1962), p. 122.

15. Claude, *Power and International Relations*, p. 91.

16. Edward Vose Gulick, *Europe's Classical Balance of Power* (New York: Norton, 1955).

17. Waltz, *Theory of International Politics*, pp. 118–119.

18. Ibid., p. 119.

19. John J. Mearsheimer, *The Tragedy of Great Power Politics* (New York: Norton, 2001), p. 139.

20. Waltz, *Theory of International Politics*, pp. 170–171.

21. Morgenthau, *Politics Among Nations*, pp. 117–155.

22. Waltz, *Theory of International Politics*, p. 131.

23. Mearsheimer, *Tragedy of Great Power Politics*, pp. 60-61.

24. Ibid., p. 56.

25. Ibid., pp. 83-84 and pp. 133-135.

26. Walt, *Origins of Alliances*, pp. 21-28. See also Stephen M. Walt, "Alliance Formation and the Balance of World Power," *International Security* 9, no. 4 (Spring 1995), pp. 9-13. Walt focuses on regional powers rather than superpowers, and the dependent variable is alliance formation rather than internal generation of power. I use a generic form of threat theory that employs Walt's independent variable of threat and focuses on balancing by internal means among superpowers. See also Stephen M. Walt, "Testing Theories of Alliance Formation: The Case of Southwest Asia," *International Organization* 42, no. 2 (Spring 1988); *Revolution and War* (Ithaca: Cornell University Press, 1996); "Containing Rogues and Renegades: Coalition Strategies and Counterproliferation," in *The Coming Crisis: Nuclear Proliferation, U.S. Interests, and World Order*, ed. Victor Utgoff (Cambridge, MA: MIT Press, 2000); Robert G. Kaufman, "To Balance or to Bandwagon? Alignment Decisions in 1930s Europe," *Security Studies* 1, no. 3 (1992); and Randall Schweller, "Bandwagoning for Profit: Bringing the Revisionist State Back In," *International Security* 19, no. 1 (Summer 1994).

27. Walt, *Origins of Alliances*, p. 24.

28. Ibid., p. 165, fn. 38.

29. Ibid., p. 165.

30. Ibid., pp. 21-26 and 147-172.

31. Walt, *Origins of Alliances*, pp. 276-279. What of geographic proximity? I am focused on superpowers with global interests where Walt is focused on alliance decisions made by non-superpowers.

32. Robert Jervis, "Cooperation Under the Security Dilemma," *World Politics* 30, no. 2 (1978), p. 187.

33. George H. Quester, *Offense and Defense in the International System* (New York: Wiley, 1977).

34. Stephen Van Evera, *Causes of War: Power and the Roots of Conflict* (Ithaca: Cornell University Press, 1999).

35. Ibid., pp. 164-166.

Chapter Two

Balance of Power: Population, Military Personnel, and Economic Resources

Balance of power argues that the US balanced against the Soviet Union because the latter was more powerful in terms of material resources. The material resources of interest to balance of power include population, military personnel, economic size and sophistication, and military expenditures.[1] These are resources that a country can use to produce its desired military program within limits of feasibility: a country with a large, sophisticated economy with a large population can choose its military program from a much broader variety than a country with a small, unsophisticated economy and a small population. This chapter considers population, military personnel, and economic size and sophistication. The next chapter assesses military expenditures.

If balance of power is correct, the Soviet Union was more powerful than the US. Balance of power would also be fortified if the Warsaw Pact was more powerful than the West. Balance of power will be infirmed if the US was more powerful than the Soviet Union or if the West was more powerful than the Warsaw Pact. Inasmuch as US balancing intensified in 1980, the relationship between US and Soviet power and between the power of the West and that of the Warsaw Pact should be one of relative change in favor of the Soviet Union and the Warsaw Pact.

POPULATION AND MILITARY PERSONNEL

While the Soviet Union's population of 265.5 million was larger than the US population of 221.6 million, the population of NATO countries of almost 572 million was much larger than the population of the Warsaw Pact countries of 375 million in 1980. Soviet active military personnel of 4.2 million[2] exceeded

America's 2.09 million and the Warsaw Pact active military personnel of 5.4 million exceeded NATO's five million. However, about 500,000 Soviet personnel faced China's more than four million[3] and 510,000 more Soviet personnel were employed in strategic offensive and defensive forces than in the US.[4] The Soviet Union also had a large number of reserve personnel comprised of recently released draftees. Soviet reserves of perhaps five million dwarfed US reserves of about 818,000, and Warsaw Pact reserves of 7.1 million were substantially larger than NATO reserves of 4.3 million. However, if Chinese reserves of perhaps 4.4 million are included among Soviet worries, the 12.5 million total active and reserve military personnel in the Warsaw Pact faced the roughly eighteen million in the forces of the West and China.[5]

ECONOMIC RESOURCES

Economic size and sophistication are critical elements of power because a large, sophisticated economy can generate and maintain larger, more sophisticated military forces than one that is smaller and less sophisticated. How did the size and sophistication of the US and Soviet economies compare in the 1970s? I begin by discussing national income, per capita national income, and economic growth as metrics of economic size and sophistication. I next consider US and Soviet GNP and per capita GNP. I then assess US and Soviet economic growth.

Metrics

The economic dimensions of power can be measured in modern economies by national income accounting. The aggregate size and growth of an economy is generally measured as GNP or GDP (hereafter I use GDP in theoretical discussions).[6] GDP is not unproblematic- it is an estimated measure, and comparisons between economies in time and space are difficult because of the index number problem. The per capita size of an economy provides an approximate measure of the sophistication of an economy through productivity, or output per hour worked, which is higher by definition as per capita GDP increases. The Solow-Denison model of economic growth explains increases in productivity by increases in the quality of the labor force and capital stock and the level of technology, factors that compose sophistication. A country with higher per capita GDP can generally replicate the technology and educational attainment of a country with lower per capita GDP while the reverse is not true.

GDP and per capita GDP constrain military elements of power. GDP limits a country's possible military expenditures at a particular time because, without borrowing or foreign transfers, a country cannot have military expenditures larger than a large percentage of its GDP. Per capita GDP does not absolutely limit per-soldier military expenditures because it is an average number and a country will have technology and an educated portion of its population beyond the average represented by per capita GDP. Per capita GDP should be understood as a range because there may be "pockets of excellence" at the high end of the range. That said, "pockets of excellence" are no more than pockets so the average is meaningful. Moreover, a country with a higher per capita GDP will have its own "pockets of excellence," and these may be beyond the reach of countries with lower per capita GDP while most of those available to the latter will generally be available to one with higher per capita GDP.

A critical source of dynamism in the distribution of power is economic growth. As economic size and sophistication today constrains the supply of military elements of power today, economic growth affects power tomorrow. A slight difference in growth rates can have profound consequences in the future: an economy growing one percent in real terms will double in size in seventy-two years while one growing two percent will double in size in thirty-six years and will quadruple in seventy-two. Thus, the yearly measures of economic power are data points over a long run that compose an economic trajectory. As a country grows it may be able to devote additional resources to military capability and if it declines it will be able to spend less. A small actual military burden (the percentage of GDP devoted to military expenditures) may allow an economy to invest resources to increase future growth and sophistication, thus allowing for a larger, more sophisticated military in the future while maintaining some surge capacity to generate military forces to the extent that its military can absorb them. In contrast, a large actual military burden may absorb capital and labor that might otherwise be used in ways that contribute to the growth and increasing sophistication of an economy. However, though intuitively sensible, these limits are poorly determined and the tradeoff relationship between military expenditures and economic growth is ambiguous.[7]

GNP

US GNP was $2.05 trillion in current dollars in 1977.[8] CIA estimated in 1982 that Soviet GNP in 1977 was 497 billion 1970 rubles, and it estimated in 1990 that Soviet GNP in 1977 was 610 billion 1982 rubles.[9]

Where estimating the size of the US economy was straightforward, any attempt to analyze the Soviet Union's secretive command economy using orthodox Western concepts faced formidable obstacles. Soviet prices were problematic because they were set administratively on the basis of Marxian labor theory of value rather than in a market that showed supply-demand relationships. Published Soviet economic statistics, when available, were incomplete, inconsistent in their definitions, often did not reveal the methodology by which they were calculated, and were presented in a Marxian framework that focused on material production and disregarded services. Further complicating any attempt to estimate the size of the Soviet economy was the emergence of an increasingly important but hard to measure informal economy.

Despite these difficulties, the CIA attempted to assess the official Soviet economy by means of a massive data collection effort and an analysis of the Soviet economy using orthodox Western economic concepts.[10] It presented its assessments in the mid- to late 1970s in its annual *Handbook of Economic Statistics*, testimony of the Director of Central Intelligence (DCI, who headed both CIA and the intelligence community as a whole) before the Joint Economic Committee (JEC) of the US Congress, and articles in occasional compendia prepared for the JEC. Primarily for reasons of the scale of effort required, CIA's work provided the only detailed and consistent set of annual estimates of the Soviet economy from 1950 to 1990 that afford an alternative to Soviet official statistics.[11] However, while it used best-practice methodology, these estimates were interpretations of Soviet data with many assumptions and the results were measures of output as opposed to social welfare.

Comparison of the US and Soviet economies is difficult because of the index number problem, a statistical problem that is present in any intertemporal or international economic comparison. In a comparison of the prices of two countries or times in terms of the prices in one country or time, the comparison will tend to overstate the relative value of the other. The problem arises because, given different resource endowments, countries tend to use more of the resources that are relatively cheap in their economy — and less of those that are relatively expensive — for a given purpose. Labor was expensive in the US and cheap in the Soviet Union while technology was (comparatively) cheap in the US and (comparatively) expensive in the Soviet Union. Hence, the US economy tended to substitute technology for labor while the Soviet economy made the opposite substitution. Estimates of Soviet GNP in terms of dollars would overstate Soviet GNP because it used more labor, which was expensive in the US, and less technology. The index number problem is more severe as differences between the comparables (e.g., levels of economic development or times being compared) increase, if prices are not available or meaningful, and as the refinement of the calculation is increased. It is important to recognize that in these situations there is no single answer and neither the ruble or dollar valuations alone are "correct." Becker suggested that "The lower (ruble) comparison might be viewed as showing the difficulty the Soviet Union would have had producing the American mix in that year, compared to its considerably smaller disadvantage in producing the Soviet mix (dollar) comparison."[12]

CIA presented its comparisons of US and Soviet GNP in several forms. First, it frequently used a "geometric mean" methodology expressed in dollars[13] in an attempt to address the index number problem in a way that avoided confusion. However, the resulting number, at best, showed "the ability of each country to produce a mix of outputs that lies between the actual mixes of the two countries."[14] Given that neither the Soviet Union nor the US sought to produce such a mix, this made for false comparisons. Second, CIA occasionally estimated Soviet GNP in dollars and US GNP in rubles. One such estimate was made in 1979 using 1976 rubles and dollars. Soviet GNP in 1977 was 523 billion 1976 rubles and 1,071 billion 1976 dollars while US GNP was 1,294 billion 1976 rubles and 1,782 billion 1976 dollars.[15]

Whether measured in rubles or dollars, the Soviet economy was much smaller than the US economy in the 1970s- about half the size if the ability to produce the US output was measured in rubles and about three-quarters the size if the ability to produce the Soviet output, marketable or not, was measured in dollars. US power did not depend on its ability to produce the Soviet mix: such civilian and military goods had little value in the world market and US military capability depended in part on goods beyond the ability of the Soviet Union to manufacture. If comparisons were made in the more relevant terms of the ability to produce the US mix of goods, then the Soviet economy was far behind.

The situation was even more striking when the G-5 (the US, Japan, Federal Republic of Germany, France, and Britain) was compared with the Warsaw Pact (the Soviet Union, German Democratic Republic, Poland, Czechoslovakia, Hungary, Romania, and Bulgaria). G-5 GNP in 1977 was 3,716 billion 1977 dollars when Warsaw Pact GNP, expressed using a favorable geometric mean methodology, was $1,400 billion.[16] US GNP alone was greater than that of the Warsaw Pact, and G-5 GNP was more than 2.65 times Warsaw Pact GNP.

Per Capita GNP

The larger population of the Soviet Union meant that the difference between US and Soviet per capita GNP was larger than the difference between GNP. Soviet per capita GNP in 1977 was 2,023 1976 rubles and 5,006 1976 dollars, and US per capita GNP was 4,863 1976 rubles and 8,091 1976 dollars.[17] On a ruble basis, Soviet per capita GNP was less than forty-two percent of the US while in dollar terms it was less than sixty-two percent of the US. Regardless of whether Soviet and US GNP were measured in dollars, rubles, or as a geometric mean of the two, US per capita GNP was much higher than that of the Soviet Union and, thus, the smaller American population was much more productive than the larger Soviet one. In retrospect, this may have overstated Soviet per capita income: Penn World Table estimates Soviet per capita GDP was 36.9 percent of the US in 1977.[18]

As indicated by the disparity in per capita GNP, the US economy was more sophisticated than the Soviet economy. Analyses of relative technology levels used in industry (including military industries) and usage of energy and materials per unit of product in the mid-1970s indicated that the Soviet economy was grossly inefficient and technologically backwards.[19] The extensive and intensive centralized direction by the Soviet government made for a rigid economy poorly able to derive economic growth from the highly-educated component of its labor force. Indeed, the Soviet economy exemplified the antithesis of Schumpeterian "creative destruction" as a sort of "sclerotic stagnation" or "stagnant destruction." The result was that "by the 1970s, the USSR had the world's most advanced late nineteenth century economy, the world's biggest and best, most inflexible rust belt."[20] In contrast, the US market economy was able to generate and employ technology and provided significant incentives for its labor force to seek higher education and to employ education and technology for self-benefit that increased the sophistication of the US economy as a whole.

ECONOMIC GROWTH

The US and Soviet economies grew at a similar rate in the 1970s but Soviet growth was expected to slow in the 1980s because of structural factors. US GDP grew almost three percent per annum in real terms between 1971 and 1980.[21] Growth was slower, about 2.3 percent, between 1971 and 1975, and faster between 1976 and 1979, about 4.4 percent.[22] Official Soviet economic statistics and CIA estimates showed Soviet GNP growth as slowing since 1960, and CIA predicted that it would continue to slow in the 1980s. CIA estimated in 1980 that Soviet GNP grew about 3.7 percent between 1971 and 1975, and then slowed to three percent between 1976 and 1979.[23] CIA consistently estimated that Soviet economic growth would continue to slow in the 1980s, with estimates in 1977 ranging from three to 3.5 percent in the early to mid-1980s with "prompt, strong action on energy policy" to two to

2.5 percent without and estimates in 1979 of two percent growth in 1985 if oil production was ten million barrels per day and one percent if oil production fell to nine million.[24] CIA estimated in 1990 that growth averaged about two percent for the period 1981-1984 in 1982 rubles; growth would have been about 2.4 percent for the same period in 1970 rubles.[25]

There are several broad explanations for the slowdown in Soviet GNP growth, each of which was used in contemporary analyses. One emphasized the limitations of extensive growth, that is, growth through increasing inputs rather than increasing productivity. Without technological change, extensive growth is ultimately limited to increases in the working population.[26] However, as discussed above, technology was no savior for the Soviet economy. A second, complementary, explanation argued that productivity was increasing slowly because of the difficulty of substituting capital for labor in the Soviet system.[27]

Contributing to both of these explanations was population growth, investment, and innovation. Soviet population growth was one percent and declining for the seventy percent of the population in Russia and Ukraine and 2.9 percent for the seventeen percent of the population in Central Asia.[28] The Central Asian population tended to be less educated, mobile, and integrated into the formal economy than their Slavic counterparts. While investment was high, it was allocated inefficiently by the visible hand of state planners and much of it was wasted in the heavily bureaucratized economy. Finally, technological innovation was inhibited by the Soviet command economy. In terms of the Solow-Denison model, this last issue probably overwhelmed quantity of capital and quality of labor and so constrained growth to close to the level of population growth.

A third explanation argued that the Soviet leadership was devoting resources to the military that could be more productively employed in the civilian economy. This might be true over long time horizons, but resources released from the Soviet military might be no more efficiently employed in the short run than those in the rest of the economy so any reallocation of resources might not affect GNP growth for some time.

A fourth explanation, appearing in CIA testimony and analyses, was that the Soviet Union was encountering resource constraints, especially in oil production. CIA estimated in 1977 that Soviet oil production was likely to peak in the early 1980s and then decline sharply.[29] However, this explanation was less about the availability of oil and other resources than about Soviet productivity and so was an intermediate rather than a primary explanation. Additionally, CIA's resource constraint explanation did not address how the Soviet Union might adapt to mitigate the expected effects.[30]

Common to these explanations was that the slowdown in Soviet GNP growth was structural rather than cyclical. Explanations that attributed the slowdown to the inefficiencies inherent in an administrative economy or to the Soviet economy's reliance on extensive growth pointed to causes that could not be readily addressed by the Soviet leadership. The military burden explanations also pointed to structural issues both because implicit in it was a claim that resources released from the military would be employed more efficiently in the civilian sector and because Soviet military spending might have such a call on resources as to make this a practically structural explanation at least through the period of leadership transition that was visible in the late 1970s. The resource constraints explanation was also structural inasmuch as it was the manifestation of productivity problems in resource production rather than availability of resources themselves.

The slowdown of Soviet GNP growth and its apparent structural nature were primary themes of CIA's public assessments of the Soviet economy and testimony by the two DCIs, George Bush and Stansfield Turner, before the JEC between 1976 and 1980.[31] The explanations of this slowdown varied. In 1976, Bush's oral testimony focused on agriculture while his written statement focused on limitations inherent in extensive growth and military spending. Turner increasingly focused on oil production. In the long term, a reduction in the growth of the Soviet labor force, diminishing returns to a slowly growing capital stock and little growth in efficiency of resource utilization, and an energy shortage would accelerate the downward trend in the rate of GNP growth expected by CIA.[32]

CIA estimated that the prospects for the Soviet economy were bleak but not catastrophic: Turner concluded his 1978 testimony by stating that reduced growth "would hardly signal the collapse of the Soviet Union and should not be perceived as a major defeat by the Soviet leadership," that absent a "powerful political leader, [CIA expected] it most likely that the Soviets will muddle through, at least into the early 1980s," and that CIA expected the Soviet leadership to:

> . . . accept a slowdown in economic growth . . . they would . . . use this period to concentrate domestic resources on renovating existing industrial capacity while making moderate changes in the administrative and managerial apparatus in the hope of stimulating future economic growth.[33]

In 1979, Turner observed that reductions in growth and investment would be economically problematic, reductions in consumption would be unpopular and would adversely affect worker productivity, and reductions in military spending risked alienating the military in a period of leadership change.

> On balance, both the present set of leaders and their successors will have to make the best of a bad situation. Short of fundamental economic reform, the

options available can only limit the impact of the economic problems rather than solve them. But wide-ranging reforms that would limit the party's control of the economy or substantially reduce the military's share of resources would be unacceptable, barring a prolonged period of stagnation and decline relative to the Western economies. Simply, no easy choices are available to any set of Soviet leaders. The ability of the new leaders to take control would depend on their ability to bite tough bullets in this area. [Security deletion] Who such leader or leaders are is a major unknown at the present.[34]

It was to be expected that the Soviet economy would grow rapidly as it recovered from the ravages of World War II. After a period of rapid growth in the 1950s, it appeared that the Soviet economy might not be able to increase its rate of growth because it depended on extensive growth and it did not appear that the Soviet system could induce intensive growth. CIA generally expected that the Soviet Union would "muddle through" and did not attempt to project outcomes beyond observing that Soviet GNP was unlikely to converge with US GNP if the Soviet economy grew as slowly as expected. To the extent that the Soviet Union could not alter its economic trajectory, any convergence would occur because of a slowdown in US growth. CIA did not make the logical statement that US and Soviet GNP might diverge and did not speculate about how this might affect relations between the US and the Soviet Union.

CIA ASSESSMENTS OF THE SOVIET ECONOMY IN RETROSPECT

CIA has been accused of overstating the size, sophistication, and rate of growth of the Soviet economy.[35] At stake in these critiques was CIA's assessment of Soviet power and its long term prospects. Broadly, if the CIA had overestimated Soviet GNP, it had overestimated Soviet power.

Criticism of CIA's assessments of the Soviet economy resulted in reports by the General Accounting Office (GAO) and the House Permanent Select Committee on Intelligence (HPSCI) to the US Congress in late 1991 that found CIA estimates were reasonable under the circumstances.[36] The difference between the critics who charged that CIA had grossly overestimated Soviet GNP and the GAO and HPSCI's findings is largely about the significance of consumer welfare. Many of the critics were correctly arguing that consumer welfare in the Soviet Union was much lower than the CIA estimates indicated. HPSCI emphasized that CIA estimates should be understood as measures of production potential rather than social welfare; unlike GNP measures in market economies where economic activity is guided by decisions of firms and households that enhance their material well-being, Soviet GNP measures summarized aggregate production activities regardless of whether the goods produced satisfied consumer demand.[37] In retrospect, CIA was reasonably correct in its estimate of the size of the Soviet economy in terms of its production potential expressed in rubles and dollars and its growth prospects, and MacEachin's defense of the CIA is reasonable with respect to the 1970s.[38]

CONCLUSIONS

The distribution of population, military personnel, and economic elements of power substantially favored the US and the West. First, the population of the West was much larger than the population of the Warsaw Pact. The West had almost as many active military personnel as the Warsaw Pact, and more once Soviet personnel assigned to strategic offensive and defensive forces and those facing China were removed.

Second, US GNP was larger than Soviet GNP in terms of the latter's production possibility, and G-5 GNP was much larger than Warsaw Pact GNP. CIA measured production possibility rather than consumer welfare, and the difference between US and Soviet GNP would have been much larger if the latter had been measured in terms of consumer welfare.

Third, US per capita GNP was much higher than Soviet per capita GNP in terms of production possibility, and the difference would have been much greater in terms of consumer welfare. Regardless of how per capita GNP was measured, the smaller US population was much more productive than the Soviet population. This higher productivity indicates that the US had a more sophisticated economy than the Soviet Union, and further warrants that the US was much more powerful in terms of economic elements of power than the Soviet Union.

The situation was more ambiguous with respect to growth. The Soviet economy was growing slowly and had little prospect of increasing its growth rate over long periods of time; while the US economy was troubled, much of its growth originated in increases in productivity so it had the possibility of faster future growth and higher long term growth potential. CIA estimated in the mid-1970s that Soviet GNP was reaching the limits of extensive growth and was likely to encounter resource bottlenecks and so would grow between one and three percent in 1970 rubles depending on oil production. Others emphasized administrative inefficiency, the consequent slow growth of factor productivity, and the burden of military expenditures. Importantly, the Soviet economy appeared to have little prospect for moving from extensive to intensive growth. With the exception of oil production, which was derivative of productivity, these factors reinforced each other to cause the Soviet economy to grow on average about two percent over the period 1981-1984 in 1982 rubles and 2.4 percent in 1970 rubles. Although the US economy was troubled by faltering productivity, inflation, and shocks in the price of oil, its potential long term growth rate was significantly higher than that of the Soviet Union. The slowdown in Soviet economic growth appeared permanent while the US might increase growth by technological change, other productivity improvements, or by changes in property rights and the public-private incentive structure (e.g., taxes, deficit spending, and level of government regulation).

Finally, these differences were so significant that precise values were not important. The Soviet economy was about half the size of the US economy when measured in rubles and about three-quarters the size when measured in its ability to produce the Soviet mix of output, marketable or not, in dollars. In either case, the difference in 1977 was some trillion 1976 rubles and a half trillion 1976 dollars. Inasmuch as the Soviet Union was unable to produce the US mix, the smaller, ruble, size was the relevant comparison. Similarly, the productivity difference between the US and Soviet populations was measured in thousands of 1976 rubles and dollars per person. If the smaller economy of the Soviet Union was confined to two percent real growth while the larger US economy grew at two to three percent each year, the Soviet economy would fall behind. The Soviet economy was smaller and less sophisticated than the US economy, and these differences were likely to increase over time.

NOTES

1. The quantity of military units, typically divisions, is also often included in the distribution of power. I address this in chapter 5.

2. CIA, *The Development of Soviet Military Power: Trends Since 1965 and Prospects for the 1980s*, April 1, 1981, p. 38. This number excludes about one million personnel in construction, transportation, civil defense, and internal security units.

3. CIA, *China's Defense Strategy and Force Posture*, August 1978, p. 5.

4. CIA, *A Comparison of Soviet and US Defense Activities, 1971–1980*, October 1981, p. 80.

5. Unless otherwise noted, data are from International Institute for Strategic Studies, *The Military Balance 1980-81* (New York: Facts on File, 1980), pp. 96–97.

6. Both measure the value of total output of final goods and services produced or the total income produced in an economy. GNP, used by the US before 1992, measures output (or income) produced by the factors of productivity owned by citizens of a country regardless of where the factors are located while GDP measures output (or income) produced within a country regardless of whether that output (or income) was produced by citizens or foreigners. GNP and GDP were (and are) quite close for

the US because US citizens and corporations abroad earned about as much as foreign citizens and corporations in the US. GNP and GDP differ substantially in a situation like Kuwait, where GNP is higher than GDP because of income from assets abroad owned by Kuwaitis.

7. According to Easterly and Fischer, "The international evidence for adverse effects of defense spending on growth is ambiguous—see Landau (1993) for a recent survey. Landau himself (1993) finds an inverted U relationship: military spending below 9 percent of GDP has a positive effect on growth, but above 9 percent it has a negative effect on growth." William Easterly and Stanley Fischer, "The Soviet Economic Decline," *World Bank Economic Review 9*, no. 3 (September 1995), pp. 347–348. See Daniel Landau, "The Economic Impact of Military Expenditures," Policy Working Research Paper 1138, World Bank Policy Research Dept., 1993. See also Jasen Castillo et al., *Military Expenditures and Economic Growth* (Santa Monica, CA: RAND, 2001), which also finds the relationship ambiguous in its literature review.

8. "Relation of Gross Domestic Product, Gross National Product, Net National Product, National Income, and Personal Income," US Dept. of Commerce Bureau of Economic Analysis (BEA), *National Income and Product Accounts* (hereafter, NIPA), www.bea.gov.

9. CIA, *USSR: Measures of Economic Growth and Development, 1950–1980* (Washington, DC: US GPO, 1982), p. 54 and Laurie Rogers Kurtzweg, *Measures of Soviet Gross National Product in 1982 Prices: A Study Prepared for the Joint Economic Committee of the United States Congress* (Washington, DC: US GPO, 1990), p. 71.

10. Overviews of the history of this process are provided by Maurice C. Ernst, "Economic Intelligence in CIA," *Studies in Intelligence* 28, no. 4 (Winter 1984) in *Inside CIA's Private World: Declassified Articles From the Agency's Internal Journal, 1955–1992*, ed. H. Bradford Westerfield (New Haven: Yale University Press, 1995), pp. 306–308 and David M. Kennedy, *Sunshine and Shadow: The CIA and the Soviet Economy*, Harvard University Kennedy School of Government Case C16-91-1096.0 (1991). CIA's methodology is described in Kurtzweg, *Measures of Soviet Gross National Product* and Government Accounting Office (hereafter GAO), *Soviet Economy: Assessment of How Well the CIA Has Estimated the Size of the Economy* (Washington, DC: September 30, 1991).

11. Gertrude E. Schroeder, "Reflections on Economic Sovietology," *Post-Soviet Affairs* 11, no. 3 (1995), p. 206.

12. Abraham Becker, "Intelligence Fiasco or Reasoned Accounting? CIA Estimates of Soviet GNP," *Post-Soviet Affairs* 10, no. 4 (1994), pp. 318–319.

13. CIA converted rubles into dollars using the geometric mean of US-weighted and Soviet-weighted dollar/ruble ratios for the prices of goods and services in each country.

14. Imogene Edwards, Margaret Hughes, and James Noren, "US and USSR: Comparisons of GNP" in Joint Economic Committee (hereafter JEC), *Soviet Economy in a Time of Change* (Washington, DC: US GPO, 1979), p. 375.

15. Ibid.

16. CIA, *Handbook of Economic Statistics*, 1978 (Washington, DC: US GPO, 1978), p. 22.

17. Data are from Edwards, Hughes, and Noren, "US and USSR: Comparisons of GNP," p. 375.

18. SUN CGDP/US CGDP (Real GDP per capita in current international prices) = 36.86. Alan Heston, Robert Summers and Bettina Aten, *Penn World Table 5.6* (Philadelphia: Center for International Comparisons of Production, Income and Prices at the University of Pennsylvania), www.pwt.econ.upenn.edu/php_site/pwt_index.php.

19. Schroeder, "Reflections on Economic Sovietology," p. 211. Ronald Amman, Julian Cooper, and R. W. Davies, eds., *The Technological Level of Soviet Industry* (New Haven: Yale University Press, 1977), p. 47 observes that the lags were less, though still present and persistent, in traditional industries like steel and electrical transmission, and were substantial and constant or increasing in science-based industries like intermediate chemicals, control instruments, computers, and military and space technologies. See also JEC, *Soviet Economy in a Time of Change; David Holloway, The Soviet Union and the Arms Race* (New Haven: Yale University Press, 1983), pp. 134–140; John M. Collins and Anthony H. Cordesman, *Imbalance of Power: Shifting U.S.-Soviet Military Strengths* (San Rafael, CA: Presidio, 1978), pp. 31–43; and Stephen Peter Rosen, *Winning the Next War: Innovation and the Modern Military* (Ithaca: Cornell University Press, 1991), pp. 46–50.

20. Daniel Chirot, "What Happened to Eastern Europe in 1989?" in Daniel Chirot, ed., *The Crisis of Leninism and the Decline of the Left: The Revolutions of 1989* (Seattle: University of Washington Press, 1991), pp. 5–6.

21. "Gross Domestic Product Percent Change From Preceding Period," BEA, NIPA.

22. CIA, *USSR: Measures of Economic Growth*, p. 20.

23. Ibid., p. 20.

24. CIA, *Soviet Economic Problems and Prospects*, July 1977 and "Testimony of Adm. Stansfield Turner," US Congress, Subcommittee on Priorities and Economy in Government of the Joint Economic Committee, *Allocation of Resources in the Soviet Union and China—1979*, 96th Congress, June 26 and July 9, 1979 (hereafter JEC (year)), pp. 2–6.

25. Kurtzweg, *Measures of Soviet Gross National Product*, p. 8. Both official Soviet figures and CIA estimates may have overstated the rate of Soviet growth. See Abraham S. Becker, "Revisiting Postwar Soviet Economic Performance" in Kennan Institute, *Occasional Paper #283 U.S. Assessments of the Soviet and Post-Soviet Russian Economy: Lessons Learned and Not Learned* (Washington, DC: Woodrow Wilson Center, 2002), pp. 16-18.

26. Easterly and Fischer, "Soviet Economic Decline," pp. 349-352.

27. Ibid., pp. 352–360.

28. Nicholas Eberstadt, "Demographic Factors in Soviet Power" in Nicholas Eberstadt, *The Tyranny of Numbers: Mismeasurement and Misrule* (Washington, DC: American Enterprise Institute, 1995), p. 121.

29. See CIA, *The Impending Soviet Oil Crisis*, February 28, 1977; CIA, *Prospects for Soviet Oil Production*, 1977; CIA, *The International Energy Situation: Outlook*

to 1985, 1977; and Senate Select Committee on Intelligence, *The Soviet Oil Situation: An Evaluation of CIA Analyses of Soviet Oil Production* (Washington, DC: US GPO, 1978).

30. See CIA, *Soviet Oil Prospects: An Intelligence Assessment*, May 1, 1981 and CIA, *Handbook* (1992), p. 128 and p. 130.

31. "Testimony of Hon. George Bush," JEC, (1976) pp. 2–3 and p. 33; "Prepared Statement of Hon. George Bush," JEC (1976), pp. 16–17; and "Testimony of Adm. Stansfield Turner," JEC (1977), pp. 2-3. See also Turner's prepared statement, Ibid., pp. 32–36; "Testimony of Adm. Stansfield Turner," JEC (1978), p. 2 and p. 38 and "Attachment: Soviet Economic Performance" Ibid., p. 61; and "Testimony of Adm. Stansfield Turner," JEC (1979), p. 2.

32. Ibid., pp. 2–6. See also CIA, *Soviet Energy Problems and Prospects*, February 9, 1979.

33. Ibid., p. 38.

34. Ibid., p. 12.

35. See Becker, "Intelligence Fiasco or Reasoned Accounting?" and Schroeder, "Reflections on Economic Sovietology" for summaries and citations of works critical of CIA's GNP estimates. Both Becker and Schroeder worked for CIA and are responding to critics. For examples, see Anders Aslund, "How Small is Soviet National Income?" in *The Impoverished Superpower: Perestroika and the Soviet Military Burden*, ed. Henry S. Rowen and Charles Wolf, Jr. (San Francisco: Institute for Contemporary Studies, 1990), p. 15; Kennedy, Sunshine and Shadow, pp. 23–25; and Nicholas Eberstatdt, "The CIA's Assessment of the Soviet Economy" in Eberstadt, *The Tyranny of Numbers*, pp. 136–149.

36. GAO, *Soviet Economy*, p. 3 and Daniel M. Berkowitz et al., "Survey Article: An Evaluation of the CIA's Analysis of Soviet Economic Performance, 1970-1990," *Comparative Economic Studies* 35, no. 2 (Summer 1993), pp. 34–36.

37. Berkowitz et al., "Survey Article," p. 37.

38. Douglas MacEachin, *CIA Assessments of the Soviet Union: The Record Versus the Charges* (Washington, DC: CIA, 1996). The restriction is specified because I have not considered other periods.

Chapter Three

Balance of Power: National Security Expenditures and the Military Burdens

Even with its smaller economy, the Soviet Union might have devoted more economic resources to national security than the US. How much did the US and the Soviet Union spend for national security, how quickly were expenditures growing, and how much of an economic burden did such spending impose? Answers for the US are straightforward. Answers for the Soviet Union are problematic because of the tortuous process of estimating expenditures and depend on how national security is defined. Answers to the burden question are even more difficult because they depend on estimates of the size of the Soviet economy as the denominator. The following sections first discuss national security expenditures in local currencies (US expenditures in dollars and Soviet expenditures in rubles) and then the growth of expenditures and the burdens they imposed on the respective economies. The final section analyzes military expenditures in terms of a common currency (dollar estimates of Soviet expenditures and ruble estimates of US expenditures).

LOCAL CURRENCY NATIONAL SECURITY EXPENDITURES

US military expenditures appeared in extensive detail in the US budget. US spending in current dollars fell as the US withdrew from Vietnam and then increased dramatically beginning in 1980. In constant (1996) dollars, US spending ranged between lows of about $230 billion in 1976-1977 and highs of almost $400 billion during the peak US involvement in Vietnam and the Reagan administration.

Soviet national security spending was published in the Soviet budget as a single number labeled "Defense." There was no specification in the budget of what this number included and excluded. According to the Soviet budget, military spending rose from less than ten billion rubles in the early 1960s to 17.85 billion rubles by 1970 and declined to 17.2 billion rubles from 1977 through 1979. The Soviet Union denied the possibility of inflation so the value was in constant rubles revalued periodically to reflect changes in the Soviet economy. However, at all plausible dollar/ruble exchange rates, spending shown in the Soviet budget appeared much too low to fund the Soviet military program. In addition, official spending did not vary with cyclical changes in procurement of ICBMs and tactical aircraft. Skepticism was shown to be warranted when Gorbachev stated in 1989 that the defense budget that year would be 77.3 billion rubles, which was up from the 1988 official budget of twenty billion rubles but apparently down from the 1988 actual budget.[1]

The US intelligence community employed two broad methodologies for estimating Soviet military spending. The first, indirect, methodology included "fixed percentage" and "residual" methods and analyzed the Soviet budget. The "fixed percentage" method, used by the Defense Intelligence Agency (DIA) until the late 1970s, assumed that national security expenditures were a fixed percentage of the Soviet budget. Holzman calculated that the fixed percent that DIA used was 32.4 percent between 1970 and 1980 and that it varied slightly between 1981 and 1987.[2] This approach was based on a statement made by Brezhnev in the early 1970s that Soviet military expenditures were about one-third of budget expenditures.[3] The "residual" method argued that official Soviet economic and budgetary data included all Soviet military expenditures; military expenditures were not labeled as such, but they were included, often in the form of residuals.[4]

Where the indirect methodologies employed a macro, top-down approach, the directly-costed "building block" methodology employed a micro, build-up approach that estimated and attributed a cost to every identifiable Soviet military item and activity.[5] Some of these (e.g., military personnel, construction, and major operating costs like fuel and lubricants) could be estimated directly in rubles, and, by the early 1960s, CIA was able to estimate approximately half of Soviet military spending directly in rubles.[6] Except for Research, Development, Testing, and Evaluation (RDT&E), which used a different methodology,[7] much of the remainder of Soviet military spending was either estimated parametrically by knowing the price of one item in rubles (e.g., an aircraft) and estimating the price of similar items based on changes in the item's parameters (physical or operating characteristics) or by providing specifications of those parameters to US manufacturers and asking how much it would cost to build the item in the US and converting the resulting price into rubles. While the latter method allowed an estimate, it was no substitute for knowing ruble prices.[8]

There were several problematic issues inherent in the construction of the estimates of Soviet military expenditures. One of the most severe was that, while data for the US program was exhaustive, that for the Soviet program was not so CIA was often multiplying unknown quantities by unknown prices. In terms of prices, ruble prices were usually available only for elements of a system, like an aircraft engine, not complete systems, like an engine with an inventory of spare parts. In addition, the complexity, and thus the cost, of Soviet military equipment was underestimated until the US acquired examples of new Soviet equipment following the 1973 Arab-Israeli War. The issue of quantities is visible in CIA's estimates of the number of military personnel. Until 1980, CIA estimated personnel by multiplying the number of identified and inferred units by manning factors.[9] In 1990 CIA substantially reduced its estimate of the number of personnel in the 1980s.[10]

Each methodology had strengths and weaknesses. The indirect methods avoided the epistemological problems associated with prices and quantities faced by the direct method but faced epistemological questions of whether the categories they used captured all Soviet military spending without including non-military spending. They could be used for burden estimates but the level of analysis was high and could not say much about issues at lower levels of analysis. Additionally, there were no ruble-dollar conversion ratios that could be generated from analysis of Soviet budgetary statistics so the indirect methods could not be used to compare Soviet and US expenditures though they could serve as a check for estimates generated by the direct method. In contrast, the building block method only estimated part of Soviet military spending in rubles, relying on estimates of some elements, particularly large procurement items, in dollars that were then converted into rubles. While the building block method was sensitive to quantities and prices for elements of the Soviet military program and to ruble-dollar ratios, it did allow for increasingly refined analysis as more data became available. Within its confidence levels of ruble-dollar ratios, the building block method allowed Soviet military spending to be analyzed in terms of both rubles and dollars and so to address the index number problem in sizing estimates in which dollar estimates of the Soviet military program would tend to overstate Soviet expenditures while ruble estimates of the US program would overstate US expenditures. Additionally, the building block method could be used to estimate independently the security component of Soviet GNP and the burden imposed by security expenditures in their several definitions on the Soviet economy. Finally, the building block method allowed data to be organized into US accounts so similar activities, like the "strategic attack" mission category, could be compared for both burden and sizing estimates once expenditures had been converted into a single currency.

Soviet national security included elements without US equivalents so CIA employed two definitions of Soviet military expenditures in the late 1970s. The "narrow" definition was directly comparable to the "National defense" line of the US budget and included activities funded by Department of Defense (DoD) less foreign military assistance, outlays for nuclear weapons and military nuclear reactors funded by the Department of Energy, Selective Service activities, and the defense activities of the US Coast Guard and Soviet Border Guards. It did not include military retirement pay; space activities in the US funded by NASA; civil defense and military assistance programs, except for the pay and allowances of uniformed personnel engaged in them; veterans programs; and the cost of Soviet Internal Troops. The "broad" definition, sought to capture how the Soviet leadership might view national security expenditures and so included those for the Internal Troops, railroad and construction troops, civil defense, military stockpiling, and space activities that in the US would be funded by NASA because CIA believed that the Soviet Union put most of its effort into the military side of its space program.

Some argued that the broad definition did not capture the full cost of some Soviet practices and so understated Soviet national security expenditures. DoD's Office of Net Assessment (ONA) argued in 1975 that "There are a range of Soviet policies or practices which accord preferences to military production over civilian counterparts and, on balance, increase the opportunity cost of military activity in ways not reflected by the price structure nor captured adequately by current estimates." Examples included selective streaming of high quality human and material resources into the military sector (exemplified by military research and development), some reports of accounting practices which systematically under-priced military production, subsidies of military activities by non-military ministries (exemplified by pre-military training for youth), and costs associated with peculiar locations and climatic conditions (exemplified by the dispersal of industries and the higher costs of troops stationed along the Chinese border).[11] Other activities without US equivalents, like Soviet military personnel assisting with agricultural harvesting, tended to overstate Soviet military spending. Treatment of retiree pensions and dependent and retiree health, education, and other benefits that did not contribute to current military capability were significantly lower in the Soviet Union, creating problems in comparing US and Soviet military spending.[12] More broadly, the integration of Soviet military and society, particularly in the subordination of economic rationality to military requirements, made distinctions between military and civil sectors arbitrary. This issue and the related "cost of empire" (e.g., economic and military subsidies of the Warsaw Pact and client states like Cuba) received increasing attention in the late 1970s and early 1980s.[13]

CIA estimated in 1979 that Soviet military spending, narrowly defined, was likely to be 58 to 63 billion 1970 rubles that year and 64 to 70 billion 1970 rubles if broadly defined.[14] The 1979 estimate reflected the consensus of the intelligence community after 1976, when CIA substantially revised upwards its ruble estimate of Soviet military expenditures and converged with estimates made by DIA.

THE GROWTH AND BURDEN OF NATIONAL SECURITY EXPENDITURES

How quickly were national security expenditures growing, and how much of a burden did they impose on the US and Soviet economies? The "burden" question assesses the strains that the several definitions of military spending impose upon a country. Though these definitions span a range of activities and thus impose a span of burdens, all are domestic. With respect to the US, which had a well specified military spending program and significant separation of the military and civilian sectors, the military burden was military spending as a percentage of GNP or GDP. With respect to the Soviet Union, the first definition of the military burden was the template of US military spending imposed on visible Soviet activities as a percentage of Soviet GNP. This was an artificial process inasmuch as it used a US definition of military spending; visible Soviet activities, many of which were priced by the US; and a US measure of Soviet GNP. The advantage of this measure was that it showed the burden of competing with the US- inasmuch as Internal Troops, for example, provided domestic order, they were an expense to the Soviet Union without contributing to Soviet military capability for balance of power purposes. The second, broader, definition of military spending was an attempt to show how the Soviet leadership might perceive the burden of national security. Internal Troops maintaining order and the leading role of the Communist Party would be viewed as a national security expense by the Soviet leadership and so part of the national security burden. The third, broadest, definition of national security expenditures attempted to capture the pervasive role of national security in Soviet life and invisible expenditures like subsidies in an attempt to approximate more closely the actual burden on the Soviet Union of its security practices and how they might be perceived by the Soviet leadership.

US military expenditures were approximately five percent of GDP between 1975 and 1981 before rising to about six percent between 1983 and 1987.

From 1976 through 1981, CIA estimated that military spending, narrowly defined, was eleven to twelve percent of Soviet GNP and twelve to thirteen percent if defined broadly.[15] In 1979, DIA estimated that Soviet military spending, undefined, was eleven to thirteen percent of Soviet GNP.[16] Andrew Marshall, the Director of ONA, implicitly using the third, broadest, definition, stated in 1975 that Soviet defense activities were likely to absorb ten to twenty percent of GNP.[17] Using a residual methodology and a definition of spending like that of the narrow definition, Lee estimated in 1977 that the Soviet burden was fourteen to fifteen percent in 1975.[18] Daniel Graham, who had recently retired as head of DIA, stated in 1976 that Soviet military expenditures were about twenty percent of GNP.[19] Again, estimation of the Soviet military burden was problematic because it used estimates of Soviet security expenditures in the numerator and estimates of the size of Soviet GNP in the denominator. If either the numerator or the denominator was "wrong," the burden would potentially be higher or lower.

Until 1976, CIA had estimated that Soviet military expenditures between 1970 and 1975 were growing at about three percent with some variance for missile procurement. The 1976 revision estimated that Soviet military spending had grown at an annual rate of four to five percent since 1965, in large part because the new ruble prices indicated that high technology programs were more expensive than CIA had estimated.[20] CIA, DIA, and Marshall estimated in the late 1970s that Soviet military expenditures were likely to increase through 1985 at approximately the same four to five percent rate, varying by procurement cycles, and that the rate of growth would not slow because of the expected slowdown in Soviet GNP growth so Soviet military spending was likely to grow faster than GNP.[21] CIA undertook a major interdisciplinary research effort in 1979-1980 to project the probable evolution of Soviet military power through 1990 and judged that Soviet expenditures were likely to rise through the 1980s, though they might be slowed late in the decade by political strains resulting from economic problems.[22]

There were several reasons why Soviet expenditures were expected to increase. CIA expected expenditures to increase because increasing complexity resulted in escalating costs over the life cycles of weapons systems, a number of costly new systems would enter production by the 1980s, the Soviet Union had already committed capital resources for expansion and there was no evidence that resource were being transferred from the military to the civilian sector, the Soviet Union saw political utility in large forces, and it was concerned about the dynamism of Western military programs and the potential threat from China. CIA argued that transfer of economic resources from the military to the civilian sector would have little impact on economic growth unless accompanied by major improvements in productivity and estimated that holding military procurement and investment constant would increase GNP growth by approximately one quarter of one percent. CIA had not detected evidence that economic pressures were causing the Soviet Union to alter its military force goals.[23] DIA emphasized the commitment of the Soviet leadership to defense, the perceptions of the Soviet leadership of threats from both East and West, and the inefficacy of transferring resources from the military to the civilian sector. Marshall expected Soviet expenditures to continue to increase because the West and China were likely to increase their own expenditures in response to the increase in Soviet military capability so the Soviet Union could not rest, and because of military lobbying and pacification during the approaching leadership transition.

CIA expressed high confidence in its projection of military expenditures for up to two years and moderate confidence up to five years. Beyond five years, CIA had low confidence "because of the difficulties inherent in projecting both individual defense programs and the complex political and economic situations which the Soviets will face in the 1980s."[24]

While military expenditures could grow faster than GNP, it became arithmetically more improbable as the time period increased. In addition, while CIA might be right that a reduction in military expenditures would do little to help Soviet GNP growth, continued growth of military expenditures in a slowing economy would aggravate the Soviet economic situation. It is difficult to imagine a Soviet economy continuing to "muddle through" CIA's estimates of increases in military expenditures; given that military expenditures could be controlled while GNP growth could not, logically, the Soviet leadership would attempt to bring increases in military expenditures into line with GNP growth. As it turns out, Soviet expenditures did not grow as fast as expected. CIA did not express even low confidence beyond five years so extrapolating more than five years is beyond what CIA estimated. The large points are that it was highly probable that the growth of Soviet military expenditures would moderate in a time frame not much longer than the periods for which CIA was expressing confidence and that CIA could have expressed high confidence about such a slowdown.

Later CIA estimates show that Soviet military expenditures rose slowly until 1985 and then rose significantly until 1988. In retrospect, the burden in 1979 would have been between about 14.5 percent and about fifteen percent in 1987.[25]

Other retrospective estimates of the growth of expenditures and the burden were much higher. Using a very broad (but not "costs of empire" broadest) definition of military expenditures, Lee estimated in 1995 that military expenditures grew eight to nine percent per annum in real terms between 1970 and 1985 and the burden grew from ten to eleven percent of GNP in 1970, seventeen to eighteen percent in 1985, and nineteen to twenty percent in 1988 as economic growth slowed.[26] Robert Gates, who had served as DCI, wrote in 1996 that he "believed instinctively" that the burden was perhaps between twenty-five and forty percent.[27] Similarly, Marshall "guessed" in 2000 that Soviet GNP was never more than thirty-five to forty percent of US GNP and that the Soviet Union devoted twenty-five to thirty-five percent of GNP to military and other national power goals.[28]

Both Gates and Marshall used the broadest definition of national security expenditures and so have a larger numerator than CIA. Marshall says the burden was higher than CIA estimated in part because the Soviet economy was smaller than CIA estimated. This points to the critical role of estimates of Soviet GNP in estimating the Soviet burden. As discussed earlier, CIA estimates of the size of Soviet GNP interpreted as measures of production potential rather than consumer welfare were higher than estimates made by others who interpreted GNP in terms of consumer welfare. Marshall does not specify the basis of his statement of the size of Soviet GNP so it is difficult to interpret his statement. While Soviet national security spending would have encompassed a broader range of activities than US spending in World War II, Gates believed and Marshall guessed that the percentage of Soviet GNP devoted to national security spending was on the same order as the US between 1943 and 1945, thirty-seven percent, and hence the Soviet economy was in a kind of wartime mobilization.

COMMON CURRENCY ESTIMATES OF MILITARY EXPENDITURES

In addition to estimating Soviet national security expenditures in rubles, CIA also estimated Soviet expenditures in dollars and, occasionally, calculated US expenditures in rubles. Use of a common currency allowed comparison of the size of the US and Soviet military programs. Dollar estimates estimated what it would cost the US to purchase the Soviet military program in the US as an alternate US program and so estimated the cost of producing, manning, and operating the Soviet military force using US costs and efficiencies. Soviet personnel, for example, were paid US rates, Soviet equipment designs were costed as if produced in the US with US manufacturing efficiencies and US profit margins, and these forces were costed as if operated using Soviet practices at US costs.[29] Ruble estimates of US expenditures were calculations using ruble-dollar ratios and did not attempt to cost the US program as a Soviet alternative. Dollar estimates used the narrow definition of Soviet expenditures and the modified definition of US expenditures discussed above so US figures did not match actual budget authorizations or appropriations.

CIA estimated in 1979 that Soviet military expenditures in 1978 were 146 billion 1978 dollars when comparable US expenditures were $102 billion,[30] estimated in 1978 that Soviet expenditures in 1977 were 130 billion 1977 dollars when comparable US expenditures were $90 billion,[31] and estimated in 1977 that Soviet expenditures in 1976 were about 118 billion 1975 dollars when US defense outlays were $84 billion.[32] CIA estimated in 1975 that US expenditures amounted to some 23.4 billion rubles, about eight percent less than Soviet expenditures of 25.5 billion rubles.[33]

A significant problem with the dollar estimates was the costing of personnel because there were several interpretations of what it meant to cost Soviet personnel in dollars using CIA's approach. According to ONA, one interpretation was that they were an aggregation of the resources used in Soviet practices while a second was that they estimated what it might cost to raise the same size force using US practices.[34] CIA stated that it "derive[d] the estimates of Soviet activities on the basis of what it would cost in the United States to develop, procure, and man a military force of the same size with the same inventory of weapons...and to operate that force as the Soviets do."[35] CIA applied US pay and allowances, rations, and clothing allowances to Soviet manpower levels but not dependent health care, overseas services for dependents, and retiree benefits. In ONA's language, CIA estimates were an aggregation of the resources used by Soviet practices. But, according to ONA's logic, to populate a Soviet force with American personnel might require not only the costs included by CIA, that is, US costs of Soviet practices that related directly to military capability, but also those which reflected the non-military characteristics of US society.

However, neither conceptualization actually estimated the dollar cost of Soviet personnel practices. The US incurred the higher costs associated with attracting individuals to volunteer, the costs of dependent health care, overseas services for dependents, and retiree benefits, and the cost of providing better comfort for the operators of its military equipment. If the additional costs associated with US practices generated greater combat effectiveness then they should not have been included in the dollar estimates of Soviet military expenditures because they were not costs borne by the Soviet Union and were not producing the putative effects enjoyed by the US. Soviet personnel practices were very different from American ones so an estimate of the Soviet military program as an alternate US military program would have estimated the cost of treating and training US soldiers as Soviet soldiers. While impossible as a practical proposition to treat US soldiers that way, the very impossibility shows the difference between the two programs and the implausibility of substituting US and Soviet soldiers for each other in estimates of military expenditures. To ignore these differences by populating the Soviet military with US soldiers in an attempt to estimate Soviet expenditures was problematic because such analyses were not costing the Soviet program as an alternate US program but as a US program with different equipment.

An estimate of the Soviet military program as an alternate US program would have to recognize and cost Soviet personnel practices that were very different from American ones.[36] Career personnel, about twenty-five percent of personnel, received about ninety percent of pay while conscripts received a "token cash wage" plus food, clothing and housing.[37] A conscript would live in primitive, barely heated barracks, help gather the agricultural harvest, and would encounter or participate in alcoholism and corruption. After 1967, he would experience the cycle of *dedovschina* inter-cohort servitude that by the mid-1970s often involved theft of food, beatings, and widespread male sexual assault.[38] He would subsist on an inadequate diet that would lead to a range of diet-related illnesses.[39] There was sufficient concern about conditions of service that new regulations in 1977 required officers to assure troops in garrison of eight hours of sleep and one hour of personal time each day. A standard in the early 1980s for new barracks mandated space for a bed, nightstand, and footlocker, and an increase in the quality of food by serving fresh meat and vegetables from unit gardens.[40]

In the Ground Forces, enlisted personnel would be trained in field units rather than training depots so units would be focused on basic skills rather than large unit effectiveness and the Soviet military likely cycled through phases of readiness with the calendar.[41] While much of his time would be spent training, much of that training would be in the form of execution of battle drills and staged maneuvers, and he would rarely use the actual equipment he would have taken to war. The typical soldier did not possess a wide set of skills. A conscript would be taught a basic skill in his first six months (e.g., driving), would acquire a special skill and a related skill in his middle year, and would teach a skill in his last six months.[42] Soviet tank crews did not interchange roles so a single casualty would typically put a tank out of action, but soldiers did rotate among vehicles so crews rarely had much practice working together. In contrast to the West, where NCOs rose through the ranks and so had demonstrated some level of skill and possessed military experience, the small number of Soviet NCOs were selected from entering cohorts by draft boards, given a six-month course, and served the balance of their two-year obligation. This was beginning to change with the introduction of the rank of *praporshchik*, or warrant officer, in 1972; while helpful, the number of *praporshchiki* was small.[43] Most tasks handled by NCOs in the West were handled by officers, including troop training and leadership, and there were roughly twice as many officers in tactical units as in NATO armies.[44] About half of the Soviet officer corps was comprised of technicians doing the kind of maintenance work handled by enlisted personnel in the West.[45] Officers were well educated, often in the some 150 college-level military academies that composed about fifteen percent of the institutions of higher learning in the Soviet Union,[46] but they had little opportunity for initiative until they commanded a regiment or larger unit.[47]

Viktor Belenko, a pilot who defected in 1976, recounts conditions "not atypical of those throughout the far East" that seem unlikely to contribute to military effectiveness:

> Between 180 and 200 [enlisted] men were jammed into barracks marginally adequate for 40 . . . There were two water faucets in each barrack, the toilet was outside, and sometimes during the night men relieved themselves in their neighbor's boots. They were given a change of underwear once a week and allowed to go into the village for a steam bath every ten days, there being no bathhouse on the base.
>
> Considerable congestion in the mess hall made cleanliness impossible, and the place smelled like a garbage pit. While one section of forty men ate, another forty stood behind them waiting to take places and plates. If they chose, they then could wait in line to dip the plate in a pan of cold water containing no soap. Usually they elected simply to brush the plate off with their hands. For breakfast, the men received 150 grams of bread, 10 grams of butter, 20 grams of sugar, barley mush cooked with water, and a mug of tea. Dinner consisted of thin soup, sometimes thickened with cereal, buckwheat groats, perhaps a piece or two of fatback, and a mug of kissel, a kind of starchy gelatin. Supper was the same as breakfast.
>
> Except for a television set, no recreational facilities of any kind were available to the enlisted men (or the officers, for that matter), and there was little they could do . . . They were forbidden to listen to a transistor radio, to draw pictures of women, to listen to records, to read fiction, to write letters about their life in the service, to lie or sit on their bunks during their free time (there was no place else to sit), to watch television except when political or patriotic programs were shown, and to drink. But drink they did, in staggering quantities, for alcohol was the one commodity available in limitless amounts.[48]

Conditions were somewhat better for officers: Belenko was paid three hundred rubles per month in the early 1970s as an instructor and was guaranteed an apartment with indoor plumbing, good quality food and medical care, and he could retire at two-thirds pay at age forty. However, his first apartment literally split apart. An officer wrote in 1990 that he and his family lived in a "plywood hut" with inadequate heat, cold water in the courtyard, access only to primitive medical care, and no access to nurseries or kindergartens. Lack of food was an ongoing problem.[49]

In the navy, a sailor would typically be assigned to operate a single piece of equipment over the course of his three-year conscription period.[50] Soviet ships spent most of their time at anchor so seamen acquired little sea experience.

While important details were apparently overlooked (for example, Odom characterized *dedovschina* as a "public secret" until the late 1980s[51]), there was some awareness of Soviet practices and problems in the US. CIA discussed inter-cohort hazing, inter-ethnic tensions, alcoholism and drug use, political disaffection, indiscipline and insubordination, corruption, desertion, and suicide, among other topics, in its 1977 *Morale and Discipline Problems in the Soviet Armed Forces*. CIA characterized Soviet military morale and discipline problems as serious and showing little prospect of improvement.[52] It is striking that there was little or no apparent interest in the subject before the *Storozhevoy* mutiny in 1975,[53] and that the issue was addressed in a memorandum may indicate that the issue had not been much studied before and that this study was a singular response rather than part of an ongoing study. The statement of General Tighe, Director of the DIA, that he viewed the situation of the Soviet conscript as one of "almost total slavery" and that he would be a poor enemy[54] indicates an awareness of Soviet personnel practices at senior military intelligence levels though DIA testimony typically emphasized the strengths of Soviet forces while leaving weaknesses unaddressed.

The difference between the cost of American volunteers and Soviet conscripts was visible in CIA estimates of the ruble cost of Soviet personnel that implied much lower costs than dollar estimates at any reasonable ruble-dollar ratio. In 1978, CIA estimated that in 1977 Soviet expenditures, narrowly defined, were 58 to 63 billion 1970 rubles[55] and that there were 4.1 million personnel in the Soviet military, narrowly defined.[56] Personnel, covering military pay and allowances, food, personal equipment, medical care, travel, and military retirement, was about sixty percent of Operating Expenditures (OE), while Operations and Maintenance (O&M), covering training and maintenance, was forty percent. OE was about twenty-eight percent of total expenditures.[57] Hence, the average per-man personnel cost of a Soviet soldier in 1977 was between 2376 and 2581 1970 rubles, O&M was between 1583 and 1717 rubles, and OE was between 3961 and 4302 rubles.

This per-man personnel cost is plausible because CIA estimated in the late 1980s that the per-man cost of a soldier in a tank division for pay, food, travel, medical care, and other costs was some 1570 rubles, a number that apparently varied in earlier periods as new data was incorporated but does not seem to have been materially different.[58] CIA found in the late 1980s that the actual per-man cost of a soldier in a tank division was 1400 rubles per year.[59]

Using the ruble/dollar exchange rate of $1.471 per ruble for 1977,[60] the personnel cost of the average soldier might be some $3495 to $3796 while the cost of a soldier in a tank division would have been about $2309 per year. The O&M cost of the average Soviet soldier would have been between $2328 and $2525, and the per-man OE would have been between $5826 and $6328. In contrast, the personnel cost (without family housing) of some 2.1 million US soldiers in 1977 was $33.672 billion,[61] or about $16,000 per soldier; O&M cost was $30.857 billion,[62] or about $14,700; and the OE for an American soldier was some $30,700. While this direct conversion and comparison is problematic because it does not allow for the comparatively greater purchasing power of a ruble (for Soviet goods of Soviet quality), the substantial difference indicates that this approach to "man a military force...and operate it as the Soviets do" would have resulted in a much lower dollar estimate of Soviet military expenditures than the imputation of US pay and allowances, rations and clothing allowances, as CIA did.

What effect would this have on aggregate expenditures? CIA estimated that Soviet military expenditures, narrowly defined, in 1977 were 58 to 63 billion 1970 rubles and 130 billion 1977 dollars. Personnel costs were one-sixth of military expenditures in the ruble estimate, or 9.66 to 10.46 billion 1970 rubles; O&M costs were 11 to 12 percent, or 6.44 to 6.97 billion rubles; and OE was 16.1 to 17.4 billion rubles. At a ruble/dollar exchange rate of $1.471, personnel costs would be $14.2 billion to $15.4 billion, O&M would be $9.5 billion to $10.2 billion, and OE would be some $23.7 billion to $25.6 billion. In contrast, personnel costs in the dollar estimates were 40 percent of military expenditures measured in dollars,[63] or some $52 billion; O&M was 15 percent, or $19.5 billion; and OE was 55 percent,[64] or some $71.5 billion. Military expenditures other than OE was $58.5 billion. Assuming that CIA's building block approach was reasonable for non-Operating Expenditures and substituting dollar conversions of ruble estimates of OE, Soviet military expenditures were some $82.2 billion to $84.1 billion when US expenditures were $90 billion. *This is crude arithmetic, but the difference between CIA estimates and this revision is so large that this revision can be incorrect by a considerable margin while making the point that costing Soviet practices in dollars as an alternate military program would have yielded much lower estimates of Soviet military expenditures than the approach employed by CIA.*

The much lower dollar estimate of Soviet expenditures resulting from estimating the dollar cost of Soviet personnel practices rather than American practices practiced in the Soviet Union might be interpreted as an index number problem, and the extent of such a problem might be indicated by estimating US expenditures in rubles. In the early 1970s, CIA made rough ruble comparisons of US and Soviet expenditures and estimated that Soviet expenditures were about ten percent higher than US expenditures in rubles in 1974.[65] CIA stated that this calculation was problematic because it simply applied highly-aggregated ruble-dollar ratios designed for other purposes to US expenditures and believed that it underestimated the ruble cost of the US program.[66] The difference between Soviet and US expenditures was larger in 1977 when CIA estimated that the Soviet program in 1976 measured in dollars was forty percent larger than the US program and twenty-five percent larger if the US program was measured in rubles.[67] The larger difference between dollar and ruble estimates was presumably because CIA increased its ruble estimate of Soviet expenditures in 1976.

The 1977 statement was consistent with its earlier statements about the small effects of the index effect shown by ruble valuations of US spending, and this difference is both smaller and in the opposite direction of my calculation. The difference originates in CIA's methodology, which understated US expenditures in ruble terms. CIA estimated the ruble value of Soviet military personnel expenditures by multiplying prices (Ps) and quantities (Qs):

P of Soviet personnel in rubles X Q of Soviet personnel,

And the dollar value of Soviet military personnel by:

P of US personnel in dollars X Q of Soviet personnel

(which was the equivalent of KGB estimating US expenditures in rubles by:

P of Soviet personnel in rubles X Q of US personnel).

Such an exercise would have been as legitimate as the US methodology of estimating dollar costs by populating the Soviet force with US personnel. What CIA did not do was estimate the dollar cost of Soviet personnel practices by:

P of Soviet personnel in dollars X Q of Soviet personnel.

CIA calculated the ruble cost of US personnel expenditures by:

(P of US personnel in dollars X Q of US Personnel) X ruble-dollar ratio.

This was not a building block estimate of what it would cost the Soviet Union to buy the US program as an alternate Soviet program (nor was it ever represented that way). To do that, CIA would have had to estimate:

P of US personnel in rubles X Q of US personnel.

In sum, the CIA estimated the dollar cost of Soviet military expenditures by a building block method that populated the Soviet military with US personnel. To be comparable with the US military program, the CIA would have had to estimate Soviet military expenditures by a building block methodology that estimated the dollar cost of populating the Soviet military with Soviet personnel. To address the index number problem that would tend to overstate the dollar cost of Soviet personnel, CIA would have had to supplement its existing building block ruble estimates of the cost of Soviet personnel with a building block ruble estimate of US personnel costs.

CONCLUSIONS

While Soviet ruble expenditures were difficult to estimate, it was clear that the Soviet economy bore a heavy burden, with contemporary CIA assessments beginning in 1976 estimating a burden of eleven to thirteen percent of GNP with expenditures increasing four to five per cent, much faster than GNP growth. Some contemporary estimates were much higher: Lee estimated fourteen to fifteen percent of GNP, while Marshall and Graham estimated up to twenty percent. In retrospect, it appears that, using CIA data, the Soviet burden was about fifteen percent. Other retrospective estimates are much higher: Marshall guessed twenty-five to thirty-five percent while Gates believed it was between twenty-five and forty percent.

Where what is striking about Soviet expenditures is the heaviness of the burden they imposed, what is striking about the US burden (and that of other Western countries) is its lightness: the US burden ranged from 4.6 percent in 1979 to a peak of 6.2 percent in 1986 and averaged 5.5 percent of GDP between 1977 and 1989. The US was bearing a heavier burden as expenditures increased almost fifty percent, but not much, because GNP was growing except in 1981 and 1983.

Estimates of expenditures in a common currency provide a way to compare the costs of military programs. However, the results are sensitive to methodology. CIA's methodology, which populated Soviet forces with US personnel, estimated that Soviet expenditures were much larger than US expenditures. My approach, which converts CIA's ruble estimate of Soviet Operating Expenditures into dollars and substitutes it into CIA's dollar estimates of Soviet expenditures, indicates that Soviet expenditures were significantly less than US expenditures.

Thus, the distribution of power favored the US. The US had a larger, more sophisticated economy that could bear contemporary military expenditures much more easily than the Soviet Union. Moreover, US expenditures were larger than Soviet expenditures when the methodology populates the Soviet military program with Soviet rather than US personnel. The burden lay heavily upon the Soviet Union's smaller economy. The Soviet Union was not more powerful than the US and the Warsaw Pact was not more powerful than the West. Balance of power does not explain US balancing behavior.

NOTES

1. Noel E. Firth and James H. Noren, *Soviet Defense Spending: A History of CIA Estimates, 1950-1990* (College Station, TX: Texas A&M University Press, 1998), p. 175.

2. Franklyn D. Holzman, "Politics and Guesswork: CIA and DIA Estimates of Soviet Military Spending," *International Security* 14, no. 2 (Fall 1989), p. 105.

3. Ibid., p. 119. Holzman cites "Personal communication to author from DIA official" as his source. CIA stated in 1982 that "In 1972 [security deletion] that "every third ruble in the governmental budget goes for defense." Brezhnev [security deletion] used the words *gosudarstvenyy byudzhet*—state budget. If "every third ruble" means approximately 30 to 36 percent, total Soviet defense spending would have been between 52 and 62 billion rubles." CIA, *The CIA Approach to Estimating Soviet Defense Spending: A Research Paper*, August 1, 1982, p. 10.

4. See Holzman, "Politics and Guesswork"; Paul Cockle, "Analysing Soviet Defense Spending: the Debate in Perspective," *Survival* 20, no. 5 (September/October 1978), pp. 209–219; and William T. Lee, *The Estimation of Soviet Defense Expenditures, 1955-75: An Unconventional Approach* (New York: Praeger, 1977).

5. The process is described in CIA, *The CIA Approach to Estimating Soviet Defense Spending*.

6. Firth and Noren, *Soviet Defense Spending*, p. 24.

7. Estimates of RDT&E used open sources, satellite surveillance of facilities, and statistical interpolation to calculate the number of facilities and personnel. See Firth and Noren, pp. 219–222 and CIA, *The CIA Approach to Estimating Soviet Defense Spending*, p. 5.

8. Firth and Noren, *Soviet Defense Spending*, pp. 23–24.

9. For example, see "Statement of Adm. Stansfield Turner," in Joint Economic Committee (JEC), *Allocation of Resources in the Soviet Union and China—1979: Hearings Before the Subcommittee on Priorities and Economy in Government of the Joint Economic Committee, Part 5*, 96th Congress, First Session, June 26, 1979, p. 28 (hereafter JEC (year)).

10. CIA, *Soviet Military Manpower: Sizing the Force*, August 1, 1990, p. iii.

11. Office of Net Assessment, "Comparison of US and SU Defense Expenditures," September 16, 1975, in JEC (1975), pp. 160-162 (hereafter, ONA, in JEC (1975)). In 1988, David Epstein, Deputy Director of ONA, included the cost of transportation assets like the kinds of trucks, civil aircraft, and shipping operated in the Soviet Union

and underutilized industrial capacity available for surge capacity that he estimated added 13.2 to 20.3 billion rubles to CIA's estimate of 1982 military expenditures of 106 billion rubles. He estimated that the cost of security and empire added 60 to 103 billion rubles to CIA's estimate of 1982 military expenditures. Epstein adjusted CIA's Soviet GNP figure by including estimates for the second (black market) economy, missing wages, and fictitious or worthless output; together, these adjustments increased the size of the Soviet economy from 719.7 billion rubles to between 782 and 825 billion rubles. David F. Epstein, "The Economic Cost of Soviet Security and Empire," in *The Impoverished Superpower: Perestroika and the Soviet Military Burden*, ed. Henry S. Rowen and Charles Wolf, Jr. (San Francisco, Institute for Contemporary Studies, 1990), pp. 127–154.

12. ONA, in JEC (1975), p. 168.

13. Firth and Noren, *Soviet Defense Spending*, pp. 132–135 and pp. 146–148. See also Anthony Cordesman, "Net Assessment Appraisal," in John M. Collins and Anthony Cordesman, *Imbalance of Power: Shifting U.S.-Soviet Military Strengths* (San Rafael, CA: Presidio Press, 1978), pp. 17–18.

14. "Prepared Statement of Adm. Stansfield Turner," in JEC (1979), p. 44.

15. "Prepared Statement of Adm. Stansfield Turner," in JEC (1979), p. 44.

16. "Testimony of Lt. Gen. Eugene F. Tighe, Jr.," in JEC (1979), p. 44 and p. 77 and "Prepared Statement of Lt. Gen. Tighe," Ibid., p. 88.

17. ONA, in JEC (1975), p. 153.

18. Lee, *Estimation of Soviet Defense Expenditures*, p. 98.

19. Daniel O. Graham, "The Soviet Military Budget Controversy," *Air Force*, May 1976, p. 37.

20. Lee, *Estimation of Soviet Defense Expenditures*, p. 22.

21. "Testimony of Adm. Stansfield Turner," in JEC (1978), pp. 34-35; "Prepared Statement of Adm. Stansfield Turner," in JEC (1979), p. 52; CIA, *Estimated Soviet Defense Spending: Trends and Prospects*, June 1978, pp. ii–iii and p. 10, in JEC (1978), pp. 15–16 and p. 28; "Testimony of Lt. Gen. Harold R. Aaron," in JEC (1978), pp. 173–174; "Prepared Statement of Lt. Gen. Harold R. Aaron," in JEC (1978), p. 202 and pp. 234-235; "Testimony of Tighe," in JEC (1979), p. 79; "Prepared Statement of Lt. Gen. Eugene F. Tighe, Jr., on the Soviet Union," in JEC (1979), p. 90; and Andrew Marshall, "Sources of Soviet Power: The Military Potential in the 1980s," in International Institute for Strategic Studies, *Prospects of Soviet Power in the 1980s, Part II*, Adelphi Paper No. 152 (London: IISS, 1979), pp. 11–12.

22. CIA, *The Development of Soviet Military Power: Trends Since 1965 and Prospects for the 1980s*, April 1, 1981.

23. "Response of Adm. Stansfield Turner to written questions posed by Senator Proxmire prior to the hearing," in JEC (1978), pp. 64-65; testimony of Douglas Diamond, in JEC (1978), p. 35; "Prepared Statement of Adm. Stansfield Turner on China," in JEC (1979), p. 51; and "Testimony of Adm. Stansfield Turner, in JEC (1979), pp. 14–15 and *passim*.

24. CIA, *Estimated Soviet Defense Spending: Trends and Prospects*, August 1978, p. 9.

25. See Laurie Kurtzweg, *Measures of Soviet Gross National Product in 1982 Prices* (Washington, DC: US GPO, 1990), pp. 56–57. See also CIA, *Moscow's Defense Spending Cuts Accelerate*, May 1, 1992.

26. Lee, *CIA Estimates of Soviet Military Expenditures*, pp. 122–124.

27. Robert M. Gates, *From the Shadows: The Ultimate Insider's Story of Five Presidents and How They Won the Cold War* (New York: Simon & Schuster, 1996), pp. 318–319.

28. Andrew W. Marshall, "Holding the Bridge," *National Interest* 62 (Winter 2000/01), p. 108, fn. 2.

29. CIA, *A Dollar Cost Comparison of Soviet and US Defense Activities, 1967–1977*, p. 4, in JEC (1978), p. 129.

30. CIA, *A Dollar Cost Comparison of Soviet and US Defense Activities, 1968–1978: A Research Paper*, January 1979, p. 3. "Total, National Defense" in 1978 was 104.5 billion 1978 dollars. Office of Management and Budget, *The Budget for Fiscal Year 2001, Historical Tables* (Washington, DC: US GPO, 2000), p. 51. CIA adjusted US spending to make it comparable by, among other things, removing the cost of pensions (about $10 billion) so the CIA figure is less than the figure in the budget.

31. CIA, *A Dollar Cost Comparison of Soviet and US Defense Activities, 1967–1977*, p. 4, in JEC (1978), p. 129.

32. CIA, *A Dollar Cost Comparison of Soviet and US Defense Activities, 1966–1976*, October 1, 1977, p. 3.

33. CIA, *The Economic Impact of Soviet Military Spending*, April 1975, p. 7.

34. ONA, in JEC (1975), pp. 172–176.

35. "Prepared Statement of Adm. Stansfield Turner on China," JEC (1979), p. 45.

36. See Christopher Donnelly, "The Soviet Soldier: Behavior, Performance, Effectiveness," in *Soviet Military Power and Performance*, ed. John Erickson and E. J. Feuchtwanger (Hamden, CT: Archon, 1979), pp. 108–112; Christopher Donnelly, *Red Banner: The Soviet Military System in Peace and War* (Coulsdon, Surrey: Jane's Information Group, 1988), pp. 175–180; and David C. Isby, *Weapons and Tactics of the Soviet Army, Fully Revised Edition* (New York: Jane's, 1988), pp. 97–98 for the selection process and details about Soviet service.

37. CIA, *Military Compensation in the Soviet Union*, January 1981, p. iii.

38. William E. Odom, *The Collapse of the Soviet Military* (New Haven: Yale University Press, 1998), p. 287 and Roger R. Reese, *The Soviet Military Experience* (New York: Routledge, 2000), pp. 149–151.

39. See Richard A. Gabriel, *The Antagonists: A Comparative Combat Assessment of the Soviet and American Soldier* (Westport, CT: Greenwood, 1984), p. 53.

40. William P. Baxter, *Soviet AirLand Battle Tactics* (Novato, CA: Presidio, 1986), p. 50.

41. See Fred Kaplan, "NATO and the Soviet Scare" *Inquiry*, June 12, 1978, in JEC (1978), pp. 111–116; Donnelly, *Red Banner*, pp. 175–181; Isby, *Weapons and Tactics of the Soviet Army*, pp 113–123; Brian Moynihan, *Claws of the Bear: The History of the Red Army From the Revolution to the Present* (New York: Houghton Mifflin, 1989), pp. 337–352; Steven J. Zaloga, *Red Thrust: Attack on the Central Front, Soviet Tactics and Capabilities in the 1990s* (Novato, CA: Presidio, 1989);

and Odom, *Collapse of the Soviet Military*, pp. 286–292. For a contrasting view, see Gabriel, *The Antagonists*.

42. Major A. E. Hemesley, *Soviet Tank Company Tactics*, pp. 59–60, quoted in John L. Scherer, *USSR Facts and Figures Annual 3, 1979* (Gulf Breeze, FL: Academic International Press, 1979), p. 118, and Donnelly, *Red Banner*, p. 177.

43. See Donnelly, "The Soviet Soldier," pp. 112-113 and *Red Banner*, pp. 181–182.

44. Odom, *Collapse of the Soviet Military*, p. 287.

45. Donnelly, *Red Banner*, p. 185.

46. Ibid., p. 182.

47. US Army, *FM 100-2-1 The Soviet Army: Operations and Tactics*, July 16, 1984, p. 2–12.

48. John Barron, *MiG Pilot: The Final Escape of Lieutenant Belenko* (New York: Reader's Digest, 1980), pp. 96–104.

49. Reese, *Soviet Military Experience*, pp. 147–148.

50. Norman Polmar, *The Naval Institute Guide to the Soviet Navy, 5th Edition* (Annapolis, MD: Naval Institute Press, 1986), p. 66.

51. Odom, *Collapse of the Soviet Military*, p. 288.

52. CIA, *Intelligence Memorandum: Morale and Discipline Problems in the Soviet Armed Forces*, April 1977, p. 15.

53. The reduced crew of the frigate *Storozhevoy* mutinied at the instigation of the political officer, who might be expected to be one of the crew most dedicated to the Communist Party, in 1975. The crew first attempted to sail from Riga to Leningrad to incite insurrection to establish true communism and then attempted to defect to Sweden; according to Swedish radio monitors, some of the pilots of aircraft sent to stop the ship would have refused to destroy it. See Leonard F. Guttridge, *Mutiny: A History of Naval Insurrection* (Annapolis, MD: Naval Institute Press, 1992), pp. 290–294.

54. "Testimony of Lt. Gen. Eugene F. Tighe, Jr.," in JEC (1979), p. 81.

55. CIA, *Estimated Soviet Defense Spending: Trends and Prospects*, June, 1978, in JEC (1978), p. 19.

56. CIA, *A Dollar Cost Comparison of Soviet and US Defense Activities, 1967–1977*, p. 12.

57. Ibid., pp. 2–3.

58. Firth and Noren, *Soviet Defense Spending*, pp. 210–211.

59. CIA, *Soviet Military Finances in a Guards Tank Division*, August 15, 1989, cited in Firth and Noren, *Soviet Defense Spending*, p. 211.

60. "Exchange Rate with US$" in Alan Heston, Robert Summers and Bettina Aten, *Penn World Table 5.6* (Philadelphia: Center for International Comparisons of Production, Income and Prices at the University of Pennsylvania).

61. "Table 3.2" in OMB, *Historical Tables*, p. 55.

62. Ibid., p. 55.

63. CIA, *A Dollar Cost Comparison of Soviet and US Defense Activities, 1966-1976*, p. 2.

64. Ibid., p. 2.

65. "Testimony of William Colby," in JEC (1975), pp. 24–25. CIA, *The Economic Impact of Soviet Military Spending*, p. 7 states "To construct a ruble comparison, US defense expenditures must be converted to rubles by appropriate average ratios of US and Soviet prices for the various categories of US defense spending. According to a very rough calculation, the ruble cost of US defense programs in 1974 was about 23.4 billion rubles. Soviet outlays in 1974 are estimated at about 25.5 billion rubles—about 10% higher than the level estimated for the United States." A footnote stated that the comparison had to be "rough and dirty" because it was almost impossible to isolate prices for individual pieces of US military equipment and the available ratios were for the existing Soviet mix so there was no ratios for equipment acquired by the US but not by the Soviet Union. Proctor was the lead author.

66. Edward Proctor, "Letter to the Hon. William Proxmire," September 5, 1975, in JEC (1975), p. 90.

67. CIA, *A Dollar Cost Comparison of Soviet and US Defense Activities, 1966–76*, p. 2.

Chapter Four

Balance of Threat: US Assessments of Soviet Intentions

Chapters 2 and 3 showed that the US was more powerful than the Soviet Union and the West was more powerful than the Warsaw Pact so it is difficult for balance of power to explain why the US balanced against the Soviet Union in the late Cold War. Balance of threat theory answers this problem by arguing that the US balanced because the Soviet Union had aggressive intentions and offensive power.

The central pillar of balance of threat theory's answer is that the US perceived that the Soviet Union had aggressive intentions. The more powerful US perceived the Soviet Union as having a high propensity to attempt to compel the US and so might initiate hostilities or accept risks that might lead to war. Fearing that the Soviet Union was aggressive, the US engaged in balancing behavior.

Did the US government perceive Soviet intentions as aggressive? If it did, there should be evidence in the public statements and internal deliberations of the US government. If there is, balance of threat might readily explain why the more powerful US balanced against the less powerful Soviet Union. If not, balance of threat's claim to explanatory power will be weakened.

Whose perceptions should be considered? Balancing behavior involves alliance formation and generation of military capability so the views of leaders who control these must be considered. In the US, this is the President and the secretaries of the State Department and the Department of Defense (DoD). These (with the Vice President) compose the statutory membership of the National Security Council (NSC). In addition, I consider the views of the statutory advisers to the NSC. These include the national security adviser and the Chairman of the Joint Chiefs of Staff. Before the reorganization of the intelligence community in 2005, the Director of Central Intelligence (DCI), who served as both head of the intelligence community and head of the CIA, was also a statutory adviser to the NSC. In addition to the views of individuals, I also consider national security strategy statements that express the formal policy of an administration.

I also consider the views of the intelligence community. The intelligence community is comprised of the organizations in the US government charged with intelligence gathering and assessment. In the late 1970s, the community was comprised of the CIA; the National Security Agency (NSA); the State Department's Bureau of Intelligence and Research (INR); the intelligence organizations of the FBI, Treasury, and Department of Energy (DOE; before October 1977, the Energy Research and Development Administration (ERDA)); the DoD's Defense Intelligence Agency (DIA); and the Army, Navy, Air Force, and Marine Corps intelligence organizations.

I consider the views of the intelligence community for two reasons. First, consonance of political and intelligence community views will increase confidence that there was a dominant view about Soviet intentions. Second, the community regularly assessed Soviet intentions in the 11-4 and 11-8 series of National Intelligence Estimates (NIEs), and these were supplemented by occasional Special NIEs (SNIEs). NIEs and SNIEs are "the most authoritative analytic product of the Intelligence community." They are the product of a process that bring together the data available in the community, coordinates the examination and interpretation of these data by participating agencies, and produces judgments that incorporate both the consensus and the dissents of the members of the community about the subject of the estimate.[1] They were issued by the DCI in his role as the head of the intelligence community so his judgment prevailed in the text. The 11-4 estimates explicitly assessed Soviet intentions; while focused on Soviet capabilities for intercontinental nuclear warfare, the 11-8 series assessed broader Soviet intentions as well.[2] I consider NIEs and SNIEs because they articulated the community's consensus view (dominated by CIA) while allowing organizations disagreeing with the consensus to insert dissents. These estimates are a discrete set of documents that show the range and flow of assessments of a community focused on assessing Soviet intentions with access to all information collected by the US government, both publicly available and secret. Because they were prepared with some regularity, they provide a more continuous assessment than the views of individual members of the NSC and the occasional national security strategy statements.

A balance of threat explanation will be supported if there is a dominant view in the US leadership that the Soviet Union had a high propensity to compel the US and so might initiate hostilities or acceptant of the risk that attempts to compel the US might lead to war. It will be further supported if this view is dominant in the intelligence community. Absence of perception of aggressive intentions weakens balance of threat.

The following sections consider five periods. The first period assesses intelligence estimates between 1970 and 1977, the views of the Ford administration, and the last national security strategy statement of the Ford administration, NSDM-348. The second section examines intelligence estimates between 1977 and 1979, the views of the members of the early Carter administration, and PD-18, the administration's first national security strategy statement. The third section considers intelligence assessments and the perceptions of the Carter administration about the entrance of Soviet troops into Afghanistan in December 1979. The fourth examines intelligence estimates in 1980 and early 1981, the views of the members of the late Carter administration, and PD-62 and PD-63, its last national security strategy statements. The final section considers intelligence estimates in 1981 and 1982, the views of the early members of the Reagan administration, and NSDD-32, the Reagan administration's first national security strategy statement.

1970–1977

Intelligence Assessments

Estimates in the early 1970s assessed the Soviet Union as an opportunistic but prudent great power unlikely to challenge the US directly but exploring the implications of its increasing military capabilities. NIE 11-4-72 stated that continuing elements of Soviet military policy included security of the Soviet homeland, protection of the gains of socialism, and fostering worldwide awareness of Soviet military strength in support of expanding Soviet influence. The Soviet Union felt free of immediate threats and that it had earned a voice in world affairs equal to that of the US. The Soviet leadership would probably expect to be able to "exercise wider political and military options" in the developing world, especially along the Soviet Union's southern periphery.[3] NIE 11-72, written in preparation for the summit meeting at which President Richard Nixon and General Secretary Leonid Brezhnev signed the SALT I interim agreement, expected the Soviet Union to remain antagonistic because of its ideology and the world power ambitions of its leaders; in the context of Soviet gains in relative military power, the Soviet Union would "press their challenge to Western interests with increasing vigor."[4]

Assessments of broad Soviet goals played a minor role in the 11-8 series in the early 1970s. NIE 11-8-70 discussed broad Soviet goals deep in the body of the estimate, characterizing the Soviet Union as "committed to the spread of the Soviet system, hostile to the US in particular, and proceed[ing] from the premise that conflict in one form or another will determine relations between the superpowers for the indefinite future." The Soviet Union "aspir[ed] to supremacy over the US in power — broadly defined."⁵ NIE 11-8-71 and NIE 11-8-72 barely touched on broad Soviet goals, simply repeating language in the "key judgments" of NIE 11-8-70:

> The broad reasons for the USSR's energetic buildup of intercontinental attack forces are neither complex nor obscure. In the early 1960s the Soviet leaders, politically and ideologically hostile to the US, and thinking and behaving as rulers of a great power, perceived that in this particular respect were conspicuously inferior to those of their most dangerous rival, the US. Consequently, they set themselves to rectify the imbalance- to achieve at a minimum a relation of rough parity.

The three estimates argued there was no reason to believe that the Soviet leaders intended deliberately to make nuclear war; rather, military capability was an attribute of power, an instrument to support policy, and a deterrent. While the Soviet Union might like to have superiority in intercontinental nuclear forces, it was not clear that it viewed superiority as a feasible objective.⁶ NIE 11-8-71 and NIE 11-8-72 added that Soviet intercontinental nuclear forces programs were "not the product of a carefully thought out strategic plan or rationale which is undeviatingly executed."⁷

There was a growing sense of concern beginning in 1973. Seeking to explain why the Soviet Union was both pursuing détente and increasing the capabilities of its intercontinental nuclear forces, SNIE 11-4-73 was consonant with earlier estimates in its characterization of the Soviet Union as "simultaneously prudent and opportunistic."⁸ NIE 11-8-73 characterized the Soviet Union the same way, and NIE 11-3/8-74 used the phrase "pragmatic opportunism."⁹ However, unlike earlier estimates, the consensus of SNIE 11-4-73, NIE 11-8-73, and NIE 11-3/8-74 was that the Soviet Union was seeking superiority in intercontinental nuclear forces if the US allowed.¹⁰ The military organizations began dissenting from the consensus. The Air Force dissent in SNIE 11-4-73 argued that the Soviet Union was exploiting détente to "forestall[] US advances in defense technology while enhancing their own relative power position."¹¹ Discussing intercontinental nuclear forces, it was joined by the Army and Navy in NIE 11-3/8-74 in saying that:

> ... the Soviet leaders foresee a decisive shift of the strategic balance in their favor, and view the superiority they hope to achieve as an umbrella under which to pursue their conflict goals throughout the world with a decreasing risk of interference ("counterrevolution") from the United States.¹²

NIE 11-3/8-75 assessed that the Soviet Union sought global hegemony in the long run but was constrained by US choices:

Deeply held ideological and doctrinal convictions impel the Soviet leaders to pose as an ultimate goal the attainment of a dominant position over the West, particularly the US, in terms of political, economic, social, and military strength. We do not doubt that if they thought they could achieve it, the Soviets would try to attain the capability to launch a nuclear attack so effective that the US could not cause devastating damage to the USSR in retaliation. Although the Soviet leaders may now entertain some hope—and in the view of some agencies already believe—that US resolve as a strategic competitor is weakening, they know realistically that the US need not concede the USSR a superior position in the next ten years. Nevertheless, they are probably striving for a strategic posture which has some visible and therefore politically useful advantages over the US and which would give the USSR better capabilities than the US to fight a nuclear war.[13]

The Air Force was even more concerned, writing in a dissent that: ". . . there is little reasonable doubt that the Soviets are striving for general strategic superiority over the US by the end of the next decade." It assessed that successful Soviet research and development programs, particularly in directed energy, might shift the balance by 1985.[14]

Where the consensus of the estimates had grown increasingly concerned about Soviet intentions in the first half of the 1970s, a wide range of assessments burst into view in NIE 11-3/8-76 and the Team B *Report* that resulted from the Team A/Team B "experiment in competitive analysis."[15] The experiment emerged from pressure by the President's Foreign Intelligence Advisory Board (PFIAB), a group of notables independently evaluating intelligence programs and advising the president about intelligence issues. In 1969, President Nixon directed the PFIAB to make an annual assessment of the level of threat to US ICBMs to supplement the NIEs. There were substantial differences in the mid-1970s between the intelligence community's estimates and the assessments of the PFIAB, with the latter assessing the Soviet leadership as believing it was approaching "superiority" in intercontinental nuclear forces, and the PFIAB pressed for an outside panel to review estimates of Soviet intercontinental nuclear forces over the preceding ten years. The PFIAB was not mollified by CIA's internal review.[16] Personnel were chosen over the summer of 1976 for three "Team B" panels to assess Soviet missile accuracy, air defenses, and strategic objectives using the same data as available to the intelligence community.

The text of Team A's NIE 11-3/8-76, embodying the views of CIA, assessed the Soviet leadership as generating increased military capability to provide the Soviet Union with a powerful deterrent and recognition as a superpower equal to the US. The Soviet leadership believed in the eventual supremacy of their system over the US, but they were aware that the US could mobilize itself.

> We do not believe that Soviet leaders presently count on a combination of actions by the USSR and lack of action by the US which would give them, in the next 10 years, a capability for intercontinental conflict so effective that the USSR could devastate the US while preventing the US from devastating the USSR. Soviet expectations, however, clearly reach well beyond a capability that merely contin[u]es to be sufficient to deter an all-out attack.
>
> In our view, the Soviets are striving to achieve war-fighting and war-survival capabilities which would leave the USSR in a better position than the US if war occurred. The Soviets also aim for intercontinental forces which have visible and therefore politically useful advantages over the US. They hope that their capabilities for intercontinental conflict will give them more latitude than they have had in the past for the vigorous pursuit of foreign policy objectives, and that these capabilities will discourage the US and others from using force or the threat of force to influence Soviet actions.

Every other participating organization dissented. The State Department's INR agreed with this as a statement about ultimate Soviet goals but believed that the Soviet leadership had more modest expectations for their programs. The Soviet leadership knew that the US did not need to concede any meaningful strategic advantage and that they did not "entertain, as a practical objective in the foreseeable future, the achievement of what could reasonably be characterized as a "war-winning" or "war-survival" posture." Rather, the Soviet leadership sought incremental advantage and to avoid falling behind the US qualitatively and so losing the position of rough equivalence they had attained with great effort. The Defense Department's DIA, the military intelligence organizations, and ERDA believed "that the Soviets do, in fact, see as attainable their objective of achieving the capability to wage an intercontinental nuclear war, should such a war occur, and survive it with resources sufficient to dominate the postwar period"; while they did not believe that the Soviet leadership had a specific date for attainment of these objectives, they were objectives nonetheless and guided Soviet force development. Further, "…the buildup of intercontinental nuclear capabilities is integral to a programmed Soviet effort to achieve the ultimate goal of a dominant position in the world." Air Force intelligence went further, in addition emphasizing the Soviet "drive for strategic superiority" and the "strides toward achieving general military superiority over all perceived constellations of enemies and for attaining a war-winning capability at all levels of conflict." The Air Force dissent concluded that the NIE failed to grasp the essential reality of Soviet capabilities, which were the most extensive war preparations in recorded history and comparable with the failure to appreciate Germany's preparations for war and conflict in the 1930s.[17]

The Team B "Strategic Objectives" panel was staffed, by its own account, with members "deliberately selected from experienced political and military analysts of Soviet affairs known to take a more somber view of the Soviet strategic threat than that accepted as the intelligence community's consensus." Its mandate was to assess whether "a good case could be made that Soviet strategic objectives [were], in fact, more ambitious and therefore implicitly more threatening to US security than they appeared to the authors of the NIEs." It found that they were. It assessed the Soviet leadership as seeking worldwide domination, seeking strategic superiority to assist in the attainment of that goal, and engaged in a peacetime buildup of military forces 'whose only counterpart was Nazi remilitarization in the 1930s.' The Soviet leadership was seeking the kinds of goals that might be attained by war, and waging a kind of war without obvious fighting, but it had a low propensity to employ force directly against the US. Rather, the Soviet Union was generating sufficient military capability that the US would be intimidated and then marginalized so open conflict would not be necessary. Team B concluded by saying that:

Within the ten year period of the National Estimate, the Soviets may well expect to achieve a degree of military superiority which would permit a dramatically more aggressive pursuit of their hegemonial objectives, including direct military challenges to Western vital interests, in the belief that such superior military force can pressure the West to acquiesce or, if not, can be used to win a military contest at any level. The actions taken by the West to develop its political cohesion and military strength will be critical in determining whether, how, and when the Soviets press to such conclusions.[18]

In sum, the Soviet leadership was seeking global hegemony; in support of this goal, it was increasing Soviet military capability and attempting to isolate the US. However, the Soviet leadership was sensitive to the distribution of military capabilities so the choice about the future relationship of the US and the Soviet Union was ultimately for the US to make because a strong US would be difficult for the Soviet Union to compel. While it had expansive objectives, the Soviet leadership was not willing to run risks that might lead to war.[19]

Assessments of Soviet intentions in 1976 ranged from INR's estimate that the leadership was concerned about falling behind the US to Air Force's claim that the Soviet Union was like Hitler's Germany in the mid-1930s. The modal position, articulated by Team B, the military organizations, and ERDA, was that the Soviet Union was seeking global hegemony. In support of that goal, it was seeking superiority in intercontinental nuclear forces and the capability to wage nuclear warfare and dominate the postwar world. CIA occupied a comparatively moderate position that the Soviet Union was seeking the military capability to wage and survive a nuclear war and thereby greater political latitude and influence but was not seeking hegemony by force of arms. Only Air Force perceived that the Soviet leadership might have a propensity to initiate hostilities or was acceptant of risks that attempts to compel the US might lead to war and so had aggressive intentions. While no other organization viewed the Soviet Union as having benign intentions, and most assessed it as seeking the capability to compel the US in the long run, none assessed the Soviet leadership as having a high propensity to compel the US and so as likely to initiate a war or acceptant that attempts to compel the US would lead to war so none perceived the Soviet leadership as having the aggressive intentions of concern to balance of threat.

The Ford Administration

Gerald Ford became President in 1974 when Richard Nixon resigned to avoid impeachment. Over its thirty-month tenure, the Ford administration faced a series of crises and challenges. Domestically, it was faced with the aftermath of Nixon's resignation, inflation, and recession. In his first State of the Union address, Ford said: "I must say . . . that the state of the Union is not good."[20] Internationally, it was faced with the North Vietnamese conquest of South Vietnam.

Ford continued the central elements of the Nixon administration's approach to the Soviet Union. Both Nixon and Ford sought to contain and cooperate with the Soviet Union in the context of a competitive relationship, seeking "simultaneously to contain the Soviet Union, shrink its influence, and work with it as this process unfolded."[21] Ford and Henry Kissinger (who served as national security adviser and Secretary of State in both the Nixon and Ford administrations) continued the policy of détente of the Nixon administration. They also continued to negotiate with the Soviet Union about limiting intercontinental nuclear forces. Ford reached an interim agreement with Brezhnev at Vladivostok in November 1974 with which he was pleased, but he was unable to reach a SALT II agreement.

While the Ford administration was concerned about increasing Soviet military capabilities, it did not view the Soviet Union as having aggressive intentions. Rather, it sought to maintain US capabilities and constrain the growth of Soviet capabilities so that the Soviet Union would not have an opportunity to explore the implications of their new strength, especially in a crisis. The Ford NSC discussed US and Soviet capabilities extensively, primarily in the context of SALT negotiations. However, there was little discussion in the NSC of Soviet intentions outside of likely negotiating positions and bureaucratic constraints. The participants viewed the Soviet Union as a competitor with which the US had to coexist, led by a frail Brezhnev supported by a quarrelsome bureaucracy.

The position of the Ford administration is visible in its discussions about US military posture and defense policy between September 1976 and January 1977. Ford requested an assessment of the distribution of military power in September 1976.[22] The *National Security Council Study on U.S. Strategy and Naval Force Requirements*, apparently discussed at an NSC meeting on December 2 for which there are no minutes, stated that the Soviet Union was seeking a fundamental shift in the "correlation of forces" that would provide solid peacetime and crisis leverage over the US and its allies. Despite Soviet efforts, US and Soviet intercontinental nuclear forces would be roughly balanced through the 1990s because each side was determined not to fall behind. The US and the Soviet Union would also maintain a "rough equivalence" in general purpose military capability. The Soviet Union would seek to expand its influence, which might lead to confrontations with the US. In addition, the Soviet conception of vital interests was likely to expand; while the Soviet Union would continue to avoid direct military clashes with the US, it might misestimate US ability and resolve.[23] Participants in the NSC meeting on December 15 at which the final NSSM-246 *U.S. Defense Policy and Military Posture* study was discussed expressed concern about the growth of Soviet military capability but gave no indication that the participants expected the Soviet Union to attempt to compel the US.[24] The resulting NSDM-348 *U.S. Defense Policy and Military Posture* stated that the US would maintain a strategic balance with the Soviet Union that guaranteed that the US would never be in an inferior position, make an adequate contribution to the defense of Europe, and sustain a global capability to meet those challenges outside Europe that threatened vital US interests.[25]

1977–1979

Intelligence Assessments

There were several competing views in 1977 and 1978 about the relationship between Soviet ends and increasing Soviet military means. NIE 11-4-77, published three weeks after NIE 11-3/8-76 and the Team B *Report*, articulated two competing, but not diametrically opposed, views within the intelligence community. The first was that the Soviet leadership was seeking "decisive strategic superiority"; such superiority was "practical and attainable in a programmed fashion" and would advance "the Soviet objective of gaining a position of overall dominance in the world." The alternative view was that the Soviet leadership did not have a "programmatic design for military superiority but a more pragmatic effort to achieve advantages where they [could] and thus a more patient approach to a continuing, tough competition" with the US. Both views were in agreement that "The Soviet leaders' basic perception of the world still posits a struggle of two great systems, in which theirs will ultimately prevail."[26] NIE 11-4-78 assessed the Soviet Union as exploring the implications of its military power and likely to be increasingly assertive and so was closer to the second view of NIE 11-4-77. The Soviet leadership had a "deep sense of manifest destiny for Soviet power in the world" and expected to attain a position of hegemony in some areas:

> Where a palpable Soviet military preponderance can be achieved, the Soviets believe that it will, over time, encourage regional actors to seek security arrangements based on Moscow's good will, with attendant political and military concessions, especially as the alternatives of military self-help and countervailing alliances prove less attractive.

The Soviet leadership was not seeking a confrontation but was less likely to retreat in one. Soviet caution was reinforced by the upcoming leadership succession and domestic economic problems though the Soviet leadership did not foresee these trends leading to an economic crisis so grave that it would lead to fundamental change. In the lone dissent in an estimate that explicitly strove for consensus, INR believed that the Soviet leadership had an "ambivalent view of the military balance in Europe and would be less confident of the superiority of the Warsaw Pact's superiority over NATO than the net judgments of the Estimate suggest." In the view of INR, Soviet programs were intended to remedy weaknesses rather than to maintain or enlarge existing advantages.[27]

NIE 11-3/8-77 and NIE 11-3/8-78 touched lightly on broad Soviet goals. They ascribed the increasing capabilities of Soviet forces to a number of reasons other than a "programmatic design." NIE 11-3/8-77 included a number of internal factors while NIE 11-3/8-78 emphasized Soviet competition with the US and Soviet perceptions that powerful intercontinental nuclear forces conferred foreign policy advantages and superior deterrence.[28]

While the intelligence community viewed Soviet intentions as far from benign, it assessed the Soviet leadership as unwilling to initiate hostilities or run risks that might lead to war so it did not perceive it to have balance of threat's aggressive intentions. The Soviet Union was competing vigorously with the US and would avail itself of any opportunity in which the US permitted it to acquire an advantage that might shift the distribution of military capability in its favor, but that was a matter of balance of military capabilities, not balance of threat.

The Carter Administration, 1977–1979

According to Carter's national security adviser, Zbigniew Brzezinski, "Of the many foreign policy debates within the Carter Administration, that over policy toward the Soviet Union was the most prolonged and intense...In time, the debate divided the Administration, at first ideologically and eventually personally."[29] The two sides of the debate were Secretary of State Cyrus Vance and Brzezinski. Vance assessed the US and the Soviet Union as engaged in a competition that could and should be managed to reduce tensions; while of central importance, relations with the Soviet Union should not dominate US foreign policy.[30] Vance wrote in his memoirs that he believed the US faced:

> ...a powerful potential adversary with growing global interests and a compelling stake in avoiding military conflict with the United States. In my view, it was doubtful that there was a Soviet master plan for world domination, but rather an unceasing probing for advantage in furthering its national interests.[31]

Brzezinski wrote in his memoirs that by 1977 he:

> ...had become increasingly concerned about the longer-term political implications of growing Soviet military power, and I feared that the Soviet Union would become increasingly tempted to use its power either to exploit Third World turbulence or to impose its will in some political contest on the United States.

The Soviet Union had attained "broad strategic parity" and the US had accepted Soviet superiority in some categories of delivery systems in SALT I. He expected that:

> At some point, when the "objective" situation became more "historically ripe," the Soviets could adopt a more revolutionary policy, exploiting such favorable preconditions for a politically decisive test, based on an acknowledged military edge. The policy was equally well-suited to promote a prolonged process in which, stealthily, a fundamental change in the political complexion of the world would occur.

However, "this Soviet thrust toward global preeminence was less likely to lead to a *Pax Sovietica* than to international chaos" because it was "economically too weak and politically too unappealing"; while it could exploit global anarchy, it was unlikely to be able to attain the global preeminence it sought.[32]

Both perceived the Soviet Union as a problem to be managed by means of cooperation and competition but differed on the mix and the role of confrontation. Vance focused on the US-Soviet relationship as a series of loosely related problems to be addressed, and sought cooperation and eschewed confrontation. In contrast, Brzezinski tended to view US-Soviet relations as a series of closely related competitive issues and so was focused on the architecture of Soviet intentions and US policy; he tended to subordinate cooperation to ways to advance competitive goals and was willing to engage in at least some confrontation.

The differences between Vance and Brzezinski are visible in their responses to the Soviet and Cuban involvement in the war between Somalia and Ethiopia. Both state that their differences widened in 1978 over this issue, Robert Gates, who was serving on the NSC staff at the time, states that it was their first serious clash, and Brzezinski wrote in his journal in March 1980 that he dated 'things going genuinely wrong' in the US-Soviet relationship to what he perceived as US under-reaction in 1978 and said on occasion "SALT II lies buried in the sands of the Ogaden."[33] Vance wrote in his memoirs that he did not believe that Soviet activities were part of a grand plan while Brzezinski was "increasingly convinced that Soviet actions were part of a larger, well-defined strategy."[34] Brzezinski emphasized his concern about Soviet forces intensifying their presence near Saudi Arabia and perceptions by the Soviet Union and other countries in the region, including Egypt, Iran, and Saudi Arabia, of US resolve and US-Soviet "rules of the road."[35]

Secretary of Defense Harold Brown viewed the Soviet Union as a serious but manageable problem, and believed that management would reduce its severity.[36] He viewed the Soviet leadership as cautious but motivated by competition, and he was concerned about the possibility that that competitiveness might be expressed in exploitation of opportunities in the Third World.[37] Like Brown, General Jones, the Chairman of the Joint Chiefs of Staff, viewed the Soviet leadership as opportunistic but believed that the distribution of military power favored the Soviet Union so they were more likely to act than Brown expected.[38]

Jimmy Carter entered office hoping to promote human rights, relax tensions with the Soviet Union, cut nuclear weapons, and move away from a policy of containment. He stated in his memoirs that "My intention was to cooperate with the Soviets whenever possible, and I saw a successful effort in controlling nuclear weapons as the best tool for improving our relations."[39] Carter indicated how far he was from containment when he stated in 1977 that the time had come to move beyond the belief that Soviet expansion was almost inevitable but that it must be contained.[40] Yet Carter also perceived Soviet military power as potentially problematic, especially in Europe. Carter preferred force reductions on both sides; failing that, military strength would have to be maintained in concert with NATO allies.[41]

Cooperation did not extend to human rights, and Carter began criticizing the Soviet Union before he entered office and continued once in office. Carter appears to have viewed human rights and security issues as largely unrelated and there was little attempt to exploit synergies or manage conflicts between them via an integrated strategy. The Soviet leadership took a different view. It maintained an extensive apparatus to ensure its continuance in power, and an attack on this apparatus, implicit in any human rights campaign, was an attack on a pillar of the Communist Party of the Soviet Union and hence a vital interest. Where Nixon and Kissinger avoided interference in the internal affairs of the Soviet Union, Garthoff characterizes the Soviet view of the Carter administration as having made a "major and dangerous shift in [US] policy." In the words of Gaddis, the US could not "simultaneously negotiate with, reform, deter, and ignore the Soviet Union."[42]

There was a range of assessments of Soviet motivations in the Carter administration in this period. Brzezinski viewed the Soviet leadership as seeking global hegemony through exploitation of opportunities; it was willing to compete intensely with the US but was averse to outright conflict. Their willingness to initiate hostilities or run risks that might result in war with the US was low so they did not have aggressive intentions for balance of threat purposes. Brown and Jones did not see the Soviet Union as seeking global hegemony; rather, it was seeking influence, and it was opportunistic in expanding its influence. All viewed the Soviet leadership as historically conservative but willing to discover the political effects of its substantial and increasing military capability by experience. Vance differed from Brzezinski, Brown, and Jones in the extent to which he viewed the Soviet leadership as willing to cooperate with the US to mutual benefit. Carter entered office seeking cooperation with the Soviet Union but also committed to promoting human rights, and apparently insensitive to the possibility that criticism might be viewed by the Soviet Union as a kind of confrontation. Carter was sufficiently committed to human rights, and implicitly not so concerned by Soviet reactions, that he continued emphasizing them even at expense to cooperation on "power" issues. Hence, only Brzezinski perceived the Soviet Union in ways that might constitute balance of threat's aggressive intentions, and he viewed the situation as one of competition rather than conflict.

PD-18 *U.S. National Strategy*, signed by Carter in August 1977, articulated US goals as counterbalancing Soviet military power and influence in Europe, the Middle East, and East Asia by military forces, political efforts, and economic programs in concert with US allies; competing politically with the Soviet Union by a commitment to human rights and national independence;

seeking Soviet cooperation to resolve regional conflicts and reducing areas of conflict that could lead to US-Soviet confrontation; pursuing arms control; and seeking areas of cooperation with the Soviet Union in economic and social development and trade. The US would "maintain an overall balance of military power between the United States and its allies on the one hand and the Soviet Union and its allies on the other at least as favorable as that that now exists."[43]

PD-18 is not a document that implies an assessment of the Soviet Union as possessing aggressive intentions. While the Soviet Union might be militarily powerful, the US had substantial economic and political strengths and was not fundamentally challenged by the Soviet Union. The view of the Soviet Union implicit in PD-18 was similar to the view implicit in the Ford administration's NSDM-348. Both administrations were concerned about the growth of Soviet military capability. Both recognized the vulnerability of the US ICBM force and the robustness of the triad, neither perceived the Soviet Union as likely to attack, and both sought to improve US capability to reinforce deterrence. Both were pessimistic about the ability of NATO to defend Europe against a Soviet attack, and both perceived that a Soviet attack was unlikely to occur or to succeed if it did. While both were concerned about the distribution of military power, neither saw the Soviet leadership as seeking to compel the US or likely to run risks that might lead to war. Both perceived the Soviet Union as attempting to expand its influence, though opportunistically rather than deliberately.

Thus there was a range of views about Soviet motivations in the intelligence community and the Carter administration. Many in the intelligence community viewed the Soviet Union as seeking advantage and, ultimately, global hegemony, while others viewed it as competing vigorously and desiring strategic advantage but unlikely to attain it. Brzezinski shared the first view, Brown and Jones shared the second, and Carter and Vance sought a more cooperative relationship and so implicitly viewed the Soviet Union as not seeking to compel the US. PD-18 envisioned US military capability consistent with the second view while seeking areas of cooperation. No one assessed the Soviet Union as seeking to compel the US and so as likely to initiate hostilities or to run risks that might lead to war so the Soviet Union was not perceived as having balance of threat's aggressive intentions.

What would evidence supporting balance of threat look like? Brzezinski and others in the administration would have had to assess the Soviet Union as not simply aspiring to global hegemony but running risks that might lead to war. Such risks would have presumably had some basis in Soviet actions. For example, the Soviet Union might have been much more aggressive about supporting Ethiopia, introducing Soviet troops and supporting an invasion of

Somalia, and perhaps providing Soviet aircraft with Soviet pilots to support it. Or, the Soviet Union could have resumed pressure over Berlin like Stalin in 1948 and Khrushchev in 1961. Or the Soviet Union could have introduced troops into Cuba beyond the "combat brigade" that was "discovered" in 1979 but which had been there for years, or reintroduced Soviet naval forces, as it did at Cienfuegos Bay in 1970. But the Soviet Union did none of these, or any of the myriad other actions that would have run the risk of war with the US.

AFGHANISTAN

Intelligence Assessments

The introduction of large numbers of Soviet troops in Afghanistan in late December 1979 marked the culmination of a shift toward more confrontational US-Soviet relations. Afghanistan had been an increasingly visible issue in the US policy process following the April 1978 coup that brought a communist regime to power. It rose in prominence in the spring of 1979 during a military mutiny in Herat. The intelligence community began to consider whether the Soviet Union might intervene and concluded that intervention was unlikely.[44] This changed by September, when CIA estimated that it might intervene with one or more airborne divisions to protect Soviet citizens and to ensure continuance of a pro-Soviet regime in the capital, but it did not expect that Soviet forces would be used to fight insurgents. While the Soviet Union might attempt to exploit the situation for strategic gain, CIA assessed the Soviet leadership as concerned about regional stability and estimated that it would only intervene to maintain a stable, non-hostile regime.[45] This position continued through December 8, when the intelligence community began to increase its estimate of the probability of intervention, though the community could not agree about its likely scale.[46]

After the introduction of large numbers of Soviet troops in late December 1979, CIA assessed Soviet motives as opportunistically seeking strategic advantage. CIA stated on January 15 that:

> It is unlikely that the Soviet occupation of Afghanistan constitutes the preplanned first step in the implementation of a highly articulated grand design for the rapid establishment of hegemonic control over all of Southwest Asia. Rather than signaling the carefully timed beginning of a premeditated strategic offensive, the offensive may have been a reluctantly authorized response to what was perceived by the Kremlin as an imminent and otherwise irreversible deterioration of its already established position in a country which fell within the Soviet Union's legitimate sphere of influence. However, there is no reason

to doubt that the Soviets covet a larger sphere of influence in Southwest Asia or to suppose that their decision to occupy Afghanistan was made without reference to broader regional objectives. On the contrary, their willingness to incur what they almost certainly anticipated would be serious costs strongly suggests a belief that their occupation of Afghanistan would improve their access to a number of extremely lucrative targets of opportunity and might eventually lead to a highly favorable and enduring shift in the regional and perhaps even global balance of power.

The Soviet occupation was predicated on a belief that Afghan resistance would be short lived; if resistance was prolonged, the Soviet Union might attempt to coerce Pakistan or even invade it. Soviet interest in Iran was high; while military intervention was unlikely outside of extreme circumstances, they would attempt to exercise influence there.[47] The intelligence community assessed in March 1980 that the Soviet Union had acted with "careful consideration of the expected consequences and potential problems." The Soviet Union sought to expand its regional influence and reduce that of China and the West. This would help them gain naval and air facilities on the Arabian Sea and the Persian Gulf and access to regional resources, and it would encourage beliefs that Soviet cooperation was required to maintain stability in oil supplies.[48] CIA stated in April 1980 that "The possibility that Afghanistan represents a qualitative turn in Soviet foreign policy in the region and toward the third world should be taken seriously."[49] Stansfield, Turner, the Director of Central Intelligence (DCI), wrote in a cover letter to Brzezinski that he "would be a bit more categoric...in stating that the Soviets' behavior in Afghanistan was not an aberration." 'There was insufficient evidence to warrant that the Soviet Union was firmly committed to continuing as aggressive a policy as in the Third World as they had shown in Afghanistan, but the track record, as exemplified by Angola, Ethiopia, Kampuchea, and Yemen, indicates a definitely greater willingness to probe the limits of US tolerance.' "As the paper concludes, how assertive the Soviets will be in the future will very likely depend upon how "successful" the Soviet leadership views their intervention in Afghanistan to have been."[50] Observing in August 1980 that Soviet military forces were increasing their ability to invade Iran, the intelligence community assessed that an invasion was unlikely in the next few months and that a Soviet decision to do so was conditioned by their perceptions of US resolve and military capabilities. The Soviet Union might invade if it perceived "an emergent low-risk opportunity to gain the enormous economic and geopolitical advantages that control of Iran might bring" or the US was attempting to intervene militarily in Iran, there was serious instability near the Soviet border, or in response to a call for assistance from a pro-Soviet faction.[51]

CIA assessed the Soviet Union as expansionist and seeking advantage, but it was most likely opportunistic rather than deliberate and its expansionism depended upon US resolve. It is striking that CIA assessed the advantage sought by the Soviet Union as essentially regional influence rather than a way to attain First World effects by Third World actions. Expansionism and search for regional influence does not constitute a propensity to compel the US, initiate war, or run risks that might lead to war. CIA recognized that such intentions were possible but assessed them as improbable.

The Carter Administration

There were significant differences about Soviet motives within the administration. Vance assessed the Soviet leadership as addressing a regional problem though some Soviet leaders saw an opportunity to "position themselves more favorably" with respect to China and Pakistan. In addition, the Soviet leadership saw little reason to be restrained given worsening US-Soviet relations. Finally, the Soviet leadership had miscalculated the extent of opposition it would encounter, both in Afghanistan and beyond.[52]

Brzezinski had been concerned about Soviet activities in Afghanistan by the spring of 1979, and he warned Carter in May that:

> ... the Soviets would be in a position, if they came to dominate Afghanistan, to promote a separate Baluchistan, which would give them access to the Indian Ocean while dismembering Pakistan and Iran. I also reminded the President of Russia's traditional push to the south, and briefed him specifically on Molotov's proposal to Hitler in late 1940 that the Nazis recognize the Soviet claim to pre-eminence in the region south of Batum and Baku.[53]

Brzezinski's initial response to the introduction of Soviet troops in December was that a 'quick, effective Soviet operation to pacify Afghanistan would be extremely costly to the US in the region and to Carter domestically so the administration's objective should be to make such an operation costly for the Soviet Union.'[54] Brzezinski wrote Carter that the US was now:

> ... facing a regional crisis. Both Iran and Afghanistan are in turmoil, and Pakistan is both unstable internally and extremely apprehensive externally. If the Soviets succeed in Afghanistan, and [deleted] the age-long dream of Moscow to have direct access to the Indian Ocean will have been fulfilled.
>
> Historically, the British provided the barrier to that drive, and Afghanistan was their buffer state. We assumed that role in 1945, but the Iranian crisis has led to the collapse of the balance of power in Southwest Asia, and it could produce Soviet presence right down to the edge of the Arabian and Oman gulfs.

> Accordingly, the Soviet intervention in Afghanistan poses for us an extremely grave challenge, both internationally and domestically. While it could be a Soviet Vietnam, the initial effects of the intervention are likely to be adverse for us . . .[55]

Brzezinski advocated limited steps against the Soviet Union itself. He discussed Johnson's response to the Soviet intervention in Czechoslovakia[56] as if it might provide a useful indicator of what action the US should take (he characterized this in his memoirs as 'establishing the minimally acceptable US response'[57]), and wrote in his journal in late December or early January that he believed:

> . . . an adequate message to the Soviets would be conveyed by some limit on U.S. grain sales to the Soviet Union, some further transfer of advanced technology to China, and a large aid package for Pakistan. This combination, I felt, would be sufficiently punitive and strategically significant.[58]

Brown articulated a clear sense of concern when he said on February 14 that 'Soviet seizure of political control of the Persian Gulf region would be comparable to seizing territory in Western Europe or Japan because of their dependency on oil from the Persian Gulf.' The Soviet Union would be "sorely tempted" to push further, politically or militarily, to gain control of the region's oil. "If the industrial democracies are deprived of access to those resources, there would almost certainly be a worldwide economic collapse of the kind that hasn't been seen for almost 50 years, probably worse. A sudden shutoff would create economic havoc here. There's nothing our allies can do in the coming decades that would save them from irreversible catastrophe if it were cut off." Soviet control of Persian Gulf oil would make Western Europe and Japan "economic vassals" of the Soviet Union. ""Because the United States is less dependent on that oil," he said with a touch of sarcasm, "we would just face economic disruption, international chaos, and looming Soviet power.""[59]

Carter considered the Soviet intervention "to be an extremely serious development," and he maintained this view over the years.[60] He stated in public and private that the Soviet action was "the greatest threat to peace since the Second World War" and was an ominous departure in the willingness of the Soviet Union to use force outside of its own borders that positioned it to exert pressure on Pakistan and Iran. Most seriously, the Soviet Union aspired to control the region's oil and so had significant implications for the US-Soviet balance of power.[61] Carter was troubled by Soviet actions but he does not appear to have viewed the Soviet Union as attempting to compel the US.

Rather, he was concerned that the Soviet Union had engaged in aggression and might engage in further aggression, especially toward the Persian Gulf, that might have serious consequences for the US. However, the Soviet Union was sensitive to the distribution military capability so the US could dissuade it by articulating its stake in the region and generating appropriate military capability.

The administration responded to the Soviet action in several ways. First, Carter articulated what came to be known as the Carter Doctrine: "An attempt by any outside force to gain control of the Persian Gulf region will be regarded as an assault on the vital interests of the United States of America, and such an assault will be repelled by any means necessary, including military force."[62] Brzezinski had drawn Carter's attention to the Truman Doctrine that marked the beginning of the US policy of containment, and the Carter Doctrine was explicitly patterned on it. Brzezinski argued that 'the point of both was that the intrusion of Soviet forces into an area of vital interest to the US would precipitate engagement with the US and that the US would be free to choose the manner of its response.'[63] Second, the administration began to improve the ability of the US to introduce military forces into the Persian Gulf region. Third, the administration intensified US relations with China. Finally, the administration imposed a number of sanctions on the Soviet Union. The result was that the administration, in the words of Garthoff, "toss[ed] almost everything moveable onto the sacrificial bonfire of sanctions, [and] it tied the whole to the obviously unattainable maximum aim of getting the Soviets to withdraw from Afghanistan."[64]

The Carter administration was concerned about the introduction of Soviet troops into Afghanistan. Brown and Carter were concerned about Soviet Union's capability to interdict the flow of oil from the Persian Gulf, Brown was concerned that it would be "sorely tempted" to gain actual control of the region's oil, and Carter warned them not to move further. Brzezinski was apparently concerned about Soviet regional influence in South Asia. These are essentially concerns that the US could not defend its vital interests, not concerns that the Soviet leadership had a high propensity to compel the US or to run risks that might lead to war. While the Carter doctrine might help deter a Soviet attempt to actualize its advantage in the Persian Gulf, the other measures would have been feckless had the administration perceived that the Soviet leadership had the aggressive intentions of balance of threat. When limitations on grain sales, provision of technology to China, and aid for Pakistan were viewed as sufficient by the administration's "hard liner," perceptions that the Soviet Union had aggressive intentions were far away.

1980–1981

Intelligence Assessments

The range of views visible in earlier estimates continued in 1980. NIE 11-3/8-79, published in March 1980, was split between two views. CIA, INR, and NSA continued their earlier assessment that the underlying purpose of Soviet capability was to "strengthen the USSR's deterrent, to support its foreign policy, and to foster strategic stability through Soviet advantage." Though Soviet capability would be at a peak relative to US capabilities in the early and mid-1980s and would decline as US programs entered service in the late 1980s, the Soviet leadership:

> . . . probably [did] not see the present situation of approximate strategic nuclear parity as providing them with the latitude to safely confront the United States directly in areas where they perceive US vital interests to be involved. However, in areas that they believe the United States regards as less central to its interests, particularly in regions where the USSR enjoys a preponderance of conventional forces and the advantage of proximity, such as Afghanistan, the current strategic relationship probably enhances Soviet confidence that the risk of a US local or escalatory military response would be negligible.

The alternative view of DIA and the military intelligence organizations, which "disassociated" themselves from the summary volume of the Estimate in a footnote to the word "Summary," held that:

> . . . the increasing aggressiveness of Soviet foreign policy will expand as the Soviet Union's advantages in strategic nuclear forces becomes more pronounced. The Soviets may now perceive that they have nuclear superiority. As they see this superiority increase during the next three to five years, they will probably attempt to secure maximum political advantage from their military arsenal in anticipation of US force modernization programs. Moreover, the holders of this view sense that the Soviet leadership remains uncertain about the bounding of US national interests and American resolve to meet challenges to these interests. If such uncertainties continue, there is the distinct danger that the USSR may grossly miscalculate US reactions during a regional crisis and thus set the stage for a serious military confrontation between the superpowers.[65]

NIE 11-3/8-80, published in December 1980, opened with the "key judgments" of Turner, the DCI, that were uncoordinated with the intelligence community. Turner did "not hold major disagreements with the key judgments coordinated by the Intelligence Community agencies or with the basic analysis of the Estimate" but he did not believe that the estimate adequately addressed the interests of senior policymakers in several critical areas. Turner assessed that the Soviet leadership believed that victory in nuclear war was possible. The leadership was "basically pleased with the general recognition that they have achieved at least "parity" or perhaps "superiority" with the US in strategic weaponry and the acknowledgement of superpower status that this confers." However, the Soviet leadership was concerned that trends in intercontinental nuclear forces might shift against them later in the 1980s so it was likely considering acquisition of even larger forces than it might have considered in 1979 though such an effort would likely be expensive and might be constrained by economic factors. Turner concluded:

> ... we believe that the Soviets will continue to make their estimation of US resolve the primary determinant in the degree to which they conduct an aggressive foreign policy in the Third World. Their sense of strategic parity or superiority may well, however, make them judge the risks to be less than they were in the past. In short, the "window of opportunity" in the early-to-middle 1980s with respect to the strategic equation will make the Soviets more willing to be adventuresome but not so much as to "go for broke" in exploiting every opportunity that presents itself in the Third World. Their perception of the strategic balance is unlikely to induce them to undertake military action in Europe or against the United States.[66]

There was a range of views in the estimate about Soviet intentions. CIA, INR, and NSA assessed the Soviet leadership as believing that any advantage it might perceive in military capability was temporary and insufficient to confront the US where vital US interests were at stake.

> Thus, during the early-to-middle 1980s, when the Soviets strategic capabilities relative to those of the United States would be greatest, we would expect them—as in the past—to probe and challenge the United States steadily to determine at what point it will react strongly. For them to "go for broke" during the next few years would mean that they had ignored the strategic equation. We think it highly unlikely that this eventuality will come to pass. Their perception of the strategic balance is unlikely to induce them to take military action against Western Europe or the United States.[67]

The military organizations assessed the Soviet leadership as enjoying increasing confidence about the military situation and were therefore likely to be more assertive, particularly, though implicitly, in the developing world.[68] The danger was that the Soviet leadership would miscalculate about US resolve, not that the Soviet Union would deliberately initiate hostilities. However, while not confronting the US directly, the Soviet leadership had global ambitions and was challenging the US indirectly. Turner, focused more on the developing world, argued that the aggressiveness of Soviet actions there were substantially affected by perceptions of US resolve and that the Soviet Union was unlikely to act militarily in Europe or against the US. There is a certain consistency between these three assessments: they viewed the Soviet Union as competing with the US but unlikely to initiate hostilities in the First World. They differed in their assessments about Soviet assertiveness in the Third World: Turner and the military organizations were explicitly concerned about Soviet assertiveness in NIE 11-3/8-80, though Turner saw the Soviet leadership as exploiting existing opportunities while the military organizations perceived the Soviet leadership as increasingly likely to create situations they could then exploit and that they were seeking to challenge US power indirectly. CIA, INR, and NSA continued to view the Soviet Union as opportunistic but prudent about confronting the US.

The Carter Administration

The later Carter administration viewed the Soviet Union as opportunistic and competitive rather than as having a high propensity to compel the US. Carter continued to maintain that "firm" US action was required to contain the Soviet Union though he increasingly recognized the possibility that the Soviet Union might not have been seeking advantage in introducing troops into Afghanistan.[69] Brown viewed the Soviet Union as essentially opportunistic, 'exploiting existing troubles rather than creating new ones though there are enough of these troubles lying around like dry tinder, as we are now witnessing in Afghanistan.'[70] General Jones was concerned that the trends in military capabilities were providing the Soviet leadership with incentives to take greater risks.

> Even with resolute action on our part to improve our global and regional deterrent capability, the days ahead will be a period of heightened risk which will require a new steadfastness and cohesion in our country and among our allies and friends. Without such resolute action, I would be frankly pessimistic about the ability of free nations to weather the turbulent decade ahead without major economic and political dislocations.

It was 'fruitless to debate whether the Soviets were embarked on a master plan or were simply opportunistic'; rather, the US must "confront the realities of Soviet capabilities, take into account their clearly articulated sense of "manifest destiny," and take the actions necessary to deny the Soviets exploitable opportunities."[71]

PD-62 and PD-63, signed in January 1981, were a summing-up and a reference for the incoming Reagan administration. They articulated a shift of US resources from Europe and Asia to the Persian Gulf because of the threat to the US, Europe, and Japan posed by Soviet activities and potential influence in the region. PD-62 *Modifications in U.S. National Security Strategy* reaffirmed PD-18 but modified it to emphasize generation of capabilities for Persian Gulf contingencies.[72] PD-63 *Persian Gulf Security Framework* reiterated the Carter doctrine, specified that the US capability to project forces into the region would be increased and the US would develop a range of military and non-military options in and beyond the region to compensate for the current Soviet regional advantage in conventional forces.[73]

While concerned by Soviet capability and actions, neither the intelligence community nor the Carter administration assessed the Soviet Union as having a high propensity to attempt to compel the US or run risks that might lead to war. Soviet intention were far from benign, but there is a gap between intense competition and seeking advantage that might lead to war from miscalculation on the one hand and willingness to initiate hostilities or deliberately run risks that might lead to war on the other, and even the DIA/military consensus after the introduction of Soviet troops into Afghanistan did not cross it. The Soviet leadership was opportunistic, but it was respectful of US capability.

1981–1982

Intelligence Assessments

M/H NIE 11-4-78, commissioned in early 1981 by William Casey, the new DCI, characterized the Soviet leadership as confident and willing to challenge the US in the Third World. This assertiveness was likely to continue so long as it perceived Western strength as declining. The Soviet leadership still viewed any direct challenge as "extremely hazardous." "However, in light of the change in the strategic balance and continued expansion of general purpose forces, the Soviets are now more prepared and may be more willing to accept the risks of confrontation in a serious crisis . . ."[74] NIE 11-4-82 assessed the Soviet leadership as believing they enjoyed some strategic advantages over the US supportive of an assertive foreign policy and the expansion of Soviet influence.

> However, they do not believe that they currently enjoy decisive strategic advantages over the United States and do not wish a major confrontation. . . . They are unlikely to initiate military hostilities in an area of crucial importance to the United States like the Persian Gulf. However, they will seize opportunities offered by instability in the Third World to enhance their geopolitical influence . . .[75]

NIE 11-3/8-81 and NIE 11-3/8-82 focused on Soviet capabilities and probable operational approaches to nuclear warfare and do not appear to have assessed Soviet intentions.[76]

The Reagan Administration

President Ronald Reagan viewed the Soviet leadership as challenging the US and seeking global hegemony. He also saw the tremendous strength of the US economy and ideology, the weakness of the Soviet economy and ideology, and was optimistic about the potential of the US economy and ideology to challenge the Soviet Union. Secretary of State Alexander Haig perceived the Soviet Union as supporting guerilla and terrorist groups, especially in areas of vital US interest, and he sought to contain and, at times for reasons of bureaucratic politics, to confront this Soviet expansionism vigorously.[77] Secretary of Defense Caspar Weinberger was concerned about US military capability rather than Soviet intentions, characterizing US military capability at the first informal NSC meeting in 1981 as "sadly very low."[78] He continued the sentiment of this characterization in later NSC meetings, speaking of the "mess we inherited" and stating that, as of 1982, the US did not have "reasonable assurance of deterring Soviet aggression."[79] Casey, the DCI, was focused on Soviet subversion in the Third World and the possibilities of US covert action.[80] The position of national security adviser was literally marginalized in the early Reagan administration. The position was removed from the cabinet, to which Carter had promoted it. Richard Allen, the national security adviser until January 1982, reported to Edwin Meese, the president's counselor, and his office was moved to the basement while Meese occupied the office that had been used by Kissinger, Brent Scowcroft, and Brzezinski. Allen's successor was William Clark, a former judge with little background in national security affairs but a confidant who reported directly to Reagan.

There was a common concern in the Reagan administration that US military capability was insufficient, but there was also a belief that the US could remedy this. Haig and Casey perceived that the Soviet Union was engaged in subversion in the Third World, but there was also a belief that the US could successfully engage in covert actions that would counter Soviet actions and challenge perceived Soviet successes. While they were concerned about US military capability, Soviet subversion, and Soviet aspirations, the members of the Reagan NSC did not perceive the Soviet Union as seeking to attempt to compel the US and so as likely to initiate hostilities or run risks that might lead to war. It is notable that General Schweitzer, the military assistant to Allen, was relieved after stating in 1981 that the Soviet Union had attained nuclear superiority, speaking of "a drift toward war," saying that the "Soviets are on the move; they are going to strike," and the US was "in the greatest danger that the republic has ever faced since its founding days."[81] Schweitzer had spoken of the Soviet Union as if it had balance of threat's aggressive intentions; if these had been the dominant views of the Reagan administration, it seems unlikely that he would have lost his job.

The Reagan administration waited until February 1982 to conduct a formal review of US strategy.[82] At the first of two NSC meetings to discuss the resulting study, the study was briefed as saying "...we are at a time of greatest danger to our national security since World War II" but "it is unlikely the Soviets will challenge us directly in the near future."[83] The resulting NSDD-32 *U.S. National Security Strategy* stated that the Soviet Union would continue to pose the key military threats to US security during the 1980s; despite increasing pressures on its economy and the growing vulnerabilities of its empire, the Soviet military would continue to expand and modernize. The Soviet Union was aware of the catastrophic consequences of initiating military action directly against the US or its allies so war was more likely to originate in regional tensions or a conflict with a Soviet client state.

> Unstable governments, weak political institutions, inefficient economies, and the persistence of traditional conflicts create opportunities for Soviet expansion in many parts of the developing world. The growing scarcity of resources, such as oil, increasing terrorism, the dangers of nuclear proliferation, uncertainties in Soviet political succession, reticence on the part of many Western countries, and the growing assertiveness of Soviet foreign policy all contribute to the unstable international environment. For these reasons, the decade of the eighties will likely pose the greatest challenge to our survival and well-being since World War II and our response could result in a fundamentally different East-West relationship by the end of this decade.[84]

The Reagan administration articulated its policy toward the Soviet Union in NSDD-75 *U.S. Relations With the USSR*, which was signed in January 1983. NSDD-75 stated that "U.S. policy toward the Soviet Union will consist of three elements: external resistance to Soviet imperialism; internal pressure on the USSR to weaken the sources of Soviet imperialism; and negotiations to eliminate, on the basis of strict reciprocity, outstanding disagreements." The primary focus of US policy would be "To contain and over time reverse Soviet expansionism by competing effectively on a sustained basis with the Soviet Union in all international arenas — particularly in the overall military balance and in geographical regions of priority concern to the US." The US would need to convey that "unacceptable behavior will incur costs that would outweigh any gains" while genuine Soviet restraint would bring benefits to them. The US would need to modernize its military capability so that 'Soviet leaders would perceive that the US was determined never to accept second place.' "Soviet calculations of possible war outcomes under any contingency must always result in outcomes so unfavorable to the USSR that there would be no incentives for Soviet leaders to initiate an attack." The end result would be a policy that was a "serious search for a stable and constructive relationship" rather than an "open-ended sterile confrontation."

NSDD-75 portrayed the Soviet Union as imperialist and expansionist. It also portrayed it as calculating. It did not portray the Soviet Union as likely to initiate war or run risks that might lead to war. Soviet expansionism was calculated, and it was entirely possible for the US to dissuade it. Moreover, the US was powerful and the Soviet Union was vulnerable. NSDD-75 implied that the US had the resources to condition Soviet behavior, 'shaping the environment in which Soviet decisions were made.' Further, the US could reverse Soviet expansionism: it could 'promote the process of change in the Soviet Union toward a more pluralistic political and economic system,' and it could work to loosen the hold of the Soviet Union on Eastern Europe and 'keep maximum pressure on the Soviet Union to withdraw from Afghanistan.'[85]

NSDD-75 was largely written by Richard Pipes, who served on the NSC staff for the first two years of the Reagan administration. Pipes had also served as the lead author of the Team B report in 1976, which had assessed the Soviet Union as seeking worldwide domination and engaged in a buildup of military forces 'whose only counterpart was Nazi remilitarization in the 1930s.' The report had concluded that: "Within the ten year period of the National Estimate, the Soviets may very well expect to achieve a degree of military superiority that would permit a dramatically more aggressive pursuit of their hegemonial objectives, including direct military challenges to Western vital interests..."[86] While it characterized the Soviet Union as expansionist, NSDD-75 did not characterize it as seeking worldwide domination, nor did it indicate that it was engaged in a singular arms buildup. Six years after the Team B report, NSDD-75 did not indicate that the Soviet Union had attained military superiority, and it did not imply that they were likely to do so in the remaining four years of the original period of the estimate. The difference between the documents may be functional: as lead author of Team B, Pipes critiqued an input into the policy process while as lead author of NSDD-75 he was articulating US policy. The result was a document much more optimistic about Soviet ambitions and US prospects.

The intelligence assessments and national security strategy of the early Reagan administration were similar to those of the late Carter administration. While NSDD-32 was more alarmed at Soviet power than PD-62, the intelligence community and both administrations viewed war as much more likely to emerge from Soviet miscalculation. No one viewed the Soviet leadership as having a high propensity to compel the US, preparing to initiate hostilities, or willing to run risks that might lead to war. The US faced a balance of military capabilities problem, which it could resolve, not the balance of threat problem of an aggressive adversary. Indeed, there was confidence in US economic power and the ability of the US to compete with the Soviet Union and to compel it. If balance of threat's aggressive intentions are to be found, they may be in the statement in the NSC discussion of NSSD 1-82 that "The bottom line is we are helping encourage the dissolution of the Soviet Empire"[87] and the statement in NSDD-75 that it was US policy to undermine Soviet ties with Eastern Europe.

CONCLUSIONS

The intelligence community's perception of Soviet intentions moved from a benign assessment in the early 1970s through a period of alarm by some in the mid-1970s that reemerged after the Soviet intervention in Afghanistan. All except INR were concerned by the growth of Soviet capability and viewed the Soviet Union as seeking global hegemony. However, no organization perceived the Soviet leadership as seeking to compel the US or as comparatively insensitive to the distribution of military capabilities. Rather the concern was that the Soviet Union was seeking an advantageous distribution of military capability, especially intercontinental forces better able to engage in nuclear warfighting. As it attained such a "strategic advantage," it was more likely to exploit opportunities to extend its influence, its definition of its own vital interests was likely to expand, and there was an increased likelihood of war from miscalculation. Hence, while Soviet intentions were not benign, they were conditioned by the distribution of military capabilities and actualization of Soviet aspirations depended upon US decisions about how much military capability it would maintain.

The Ford administration's 1977 national security strategy did not view the Soviet Union as seeking to compel the US. There was a variety of views in the Carter administration, but even Brzezinski, the most concerned, did not view the Soviet leadership as having a high propensity to attempt to compel the US. It was an intense competitor that aspired to global hegemony, but it was not about to initiate war or willing to run risks that might lead to war. The other members of the Carter administration saw it as at most opportunistic, and Carter and Vance sought ways to cooperate. This view changed somewhat after Soviet troops entered Afghanistan, but even Brzezinski thought that reduction of grain sales to the Soviet Union and provision of technology to China and aid to Pakistan would be a sufficient response. This is not the response of someone who perceived the Soviet Union as attempting to compel the US. Ultimately, the Carter administration viewed the situation as a problem in which US ability to protect its interests was insufficient and required articulation that the Persian Gulf was a vital US interest and increased ability of the US to introduce military forces there. It was not a balance of threat problem in which the Soviet Union was attempting to compel the US despite the availability of US forces. The early Reagan administration was even more concerned about Soviet capability and NSDD-32 characterized the 1980s as 'posing the greatest challenge to US survival and well-being since World War II.' However, if war came, it would be because of Soviet miscalculation, not because the Soviet leadership had a high propensity to attempt to compel the US.

While no one assessed Soviet intentions as benign, there was not a dominant view that the Soviet Union had a high propensity to attempt to compel the US and so might initiate war or run risks that might lead to war. Hence, the US did not perceive the Soviet Union as having aggressive intentions.

What might change this assessment? Balance of threat might argue that the definition of aggressive intentions used here is actually that of hostile intentions and that Soviet expansionism and desire for influence and perhaps hegemony constituted aggressive intentions. The canonical case of aggressive intentions is Hitler and Nazi Germany. Hitler sought to conquer Europe and repeatedly disregarded the balance of power through 1941 because of his beliefs about British and French resolve and Soviet resilience. There were concerns about US resolve and resilience by some of the more alarmed observers in the 1970s, exemplified by the Committee on the Present Danger, but only Air Force intelligence assessed the Soviet Union as like Hitler's Germany, and it did so only in 1976. Every other party concerned about Soviet motives viewed the Soviet Union as opportunistic, competitive, and seeking advantage, but fundamentally unwilling to initiate hostilities or run risks that might lead to war. Moreover, no one assessed the Soviet leadership as comparatively insensitive to the distribution of military capabilities. Rather, those who were concerned about the situation focused on the sufficiency of US military capability. Hence, this was a matter of balance of military capabilities, not balance of threat.

NOTES

1. Harold P. Ford, *Estimative Intelligence: The Purposes and Problems of National Intelligence Estimating, Revised Edition* (Lanham, MD: University Press of America, 1993), p. 31.

2. After 1957, NIEs were generally designated by a two or three part code. The first group was the geographical area; for the Soviet Union, this number was 11. If relevant, the second group was a subject area; the subject code for strategic air defense was 3, main trends in military policy was 4, and strategic attack was 11. The final group referred to the year in which the NIE was commissioned. After 1973, series 3 and 8 were combined to form the 11-3/8 series.

3. NIE 11-4-72 *Issues and Options in Soviet Military Policy*, March 2, 1972, pp. 3–9.

4. NIE 11-72 *Soviet Foreign Policies and the Outlook for Soviet-American Relations*, April 20, 1972, p. 8.

5. NIE 11-8-70 *Soviet Forces for Intercontinental Attack*, November 24, 1970, pp. 55–56.

6. NIE 11-8-70, pp. 5-6; NIE 11-8-71 *Soviet Forces for Intercontinental Attack*, March 9, 1972, p. 6; and NIE 11-8-72 *Soviet Forces for Intercontinental Attack*, October 26, 1972, pp. 2–5.

7. NIE 11-8-71, p. 7 and NIE 11-8-72, p. 6.

8. SNIE 11-4-73 *Soviet Strategic Arms Programs and Détente: What Are They Up To?*, September 10, 1973, p. 3.

9. NIE 11-8-73 *Soviet Forces for Intercontinental Attack*, January 25, 1974, p. 21 and NIE 11-3/8-74 *Soviet Forces for Intercontinental Conflict Through 1985*, November 14, 1974, p. 10.

10. SNIE 11-4-73, p. 10; NIE 11-8-73, pp. 4-5; and NIE 11-3/8-74, p. 7.

11. SNIE 11-4-73, p. 4, fn. 1.

12. NIE 11-3/8-74, p. 11. Although their dissents had appeared in the meantime, this was the first time since 1963 that the Army, Navy, and Air Force were identified as distinct organizations participating in the preparation of an estimate in the 11-8 series.

13. NIE 11-3/8-75 *Soviet Forces for Intercontinental Conflict Through the Mid-1980s*, November 17, 1975, p. 5.

14. Ibid., p. 2.

15. The most complete account of the Team B "experiment" is Anne Hessing Cahn, *Killing Détente: The Right Attacks the CIA* (University Park, PA: Pennsylvania State University Press, 1998). See also Senate Select Committee on Intelligence, Subcommittee on Collection, Production, and Quality, *The National Intelligence Estimates A-B Team Episode Concerning Soviet Strategic Capability and Objectives*, 95th Congress, 2nd Session, 1978; John Prados, *The Soviet Estimate: U.S. Intelligence Analysis and Russian Military Strength* (New York: Dial, 1982), pp. 248–257; Richard Pipes, "Team B: The Reality Behind the Myth," *Commentary*, October 1986, pp. 25–40; and Anne Hessing Cahn and John Prados, "Team B: The Trillion Dollar Experiment," *Bulletin of the Atomic Scientists* 49, no. 3 (April 1993).

16. The review was Robert L. Hewitt, John Ashton, and John H. Milligan, *The Track Record in Strategic Estimating: An Evaluation of the Strategic National Intelligence Estimates, 1966–1975*, February 6, 1976.

17. NIE 11-3/8-76 *Soviet Forces for Intercontinental Conflict Through the Mid-1980s*, December 21, 1976, pp. 2–6.

18. *Soviet Strategic Objectives: An Alternative View: Report of Team "B,"* December 1976, pp. 5–6 and pp. 46–47. Italics in original.

19. Team B is a contentious subject. George Bush, the Director of Central Intelligence, stated in "public" that he thought the experiment a "worthwhile project." "Memorandum for Recipients of National Intelligence Estimate 11-3/8-76." He stated in the privacy of the last NSC meeting of the Ford administration that the idea seemed good at the time but that the views of Team B were visible in the dissents of the Air Force and he was appalled by the leaks. Kissinger made the more important point in his comment that he "could find a board of Nobel Prize winners to construct any alternative analysis conceivable. Unless you construct both the hard and soft lines it can be used by someone else for their own benefit." "Minutes, National Security Council Meeting, Semiannual Review of the Intelligence Community," January 13, 1977, p. 7, Box 2, National Security Adviser, National Security Council Meetings File, Gerald R. Ford Library.

20. "President Gerald R. Ford's Address Before a Joint Session of the Congress Reporting on the State of the Union," January 15, 1975.

21. Henry Kissinger, *Years of Renewal* (New York: Simon & Schuster, 1999), p. 110.

22. NSSM 246 *National Defense Policy and Military Posture*, September 2, 1976. Box 2, National Security Decision Memoranda and Study Memoranda, Gerald R. Ford Library.

23. NSC, *National Security Council Study on U.S. Strategy and Naval Force Requirements*, November 16, 1976, p. 6, National Security Adviser. NSC Program Analysis Staff Files, Box 2, Defense Review Panel Meeting, November 24, 1976, Gerald R. Ford Library. According to the Ford Library, there are no minutes for the December 2 meeting.

24. "Minutes, National Security Council Meeting, December 15, 1976," Box 2, National Security Adviser. National Security Council Meetings File, Gerald R. Ford Library.

25. NSDM 348 *U.S. Defense Policy and Military Posture*, January 20, 1977, Box 1, National Security Decision Memoranda and Study Memoranda, Gerald R. Ford Library.

26. NIE 11-4-77 *Soviet Strategic Objectives*, January 12, 1977, pp. 3–4.

27. NIE 11-4-78 *Soviet Goals and Expectations in the Global Power Arena*, May 9, 1978, pp. vii–xii and p. 44.

28. NIE 11-3/8-77 *Soviet Capabilities for Strategic Nuclear Conflict Through the Late 1980s, Volume I — Summary Estimate*, February 21, 1978, p. 4 and NIE 11-3/8-78 *Soviet Capabilities for Strategic Nuclear Conflict Through the Late 1980s, Volume I — The Estimate*, January 16, 1979, p. 24.

29. Zbigniew Brzezinski, *Power and Principle: Memoirs of the National Security Adviser, 1977-1981* (New York: Farrar, Straus and Giroux, 1983), p. 146.

30. See Cyrus Vance, "Overview of Foreign Policy Issues and Positions," October 24, 1976, in Cyrus Vance, *Hard Choices: Critical Years in America's Foreign Policy* (New York: Simon & Schuster, 1983), p. 441.

31. Vance, *Hard Choices*, p. 28.

32. Brzezinski, *Power and Principle*, p. 3 and pp. 146–149.
33. Robert M. Gates, *From the Shadows: The Ultimate Insider's Story of Five Presidents and How They Won the Cold War* (New York: Simon & Schuster, 1996), p. 73 and Brzezinski, *Power and Principle*, p. 189.
34. Vance, *Hard Choices*, pp. 84–85.
35. Brzezinski, *Power and Principle*, p. 178.
36. "Statement by Harold Brown, February 22, 1977," *Survival* 23, no. 3 (May/June 1977), pp. 121–124 and *Department of Defense Annual Report Fiscal Year 1979*, February 2, 1978, p. 10 (hereafter *Report* (year)).
37. Harold Brown, *Thinking About National Security: Defense and Foreign Policy in a Dangerous World* (Boulder, CO: Westview, 1983), pp. 12–17.
38. *United States Military Posture for FY 1980: An Overview by Gen. David C. Jones, Chairman of the Joint Chiefs of Staff* (Washington, DC: 1979). Jones quoted this statement in *United States Military Posture for FY 1981*.
39. Jimmy Carter, *Keeping Faith: Memoirs of a President* (New York: Bantam, 1982), p. 218.
40. Carter, "Address at Commencement Exercises at the University of Notre Dame," May 22, 1977, in *Public Papers of the Presidents of the United States: Jimmy Carter, 1977* (Washington, DC: US GPO, 1977), pp. 956-957 (hereafter *PPP*).
41. Carter, "Text of Remarks at the First Session of the NATO Ministerial Meeting," May 10, 1977, *PPP* (1977), p. 850 and "Address at Wake Forest University," March 17, 1978 *PPP* (1978), p. 531. See also "Address at the Commencement Exercises of the U.S. Naval Academy," June 7, 1978, *PPP* (1978), p. 1053 and p. 1057.
42. John Lewis Gaddis, *Strategies of Containment* (New York: Oxford University Press, 1982), p. 350.
43. PD-18 *U.S. National Strategy*, August 24, 1977, pp. 1-2.
44. Douglas MacEachin, *Predicting the Soviet Invasion of Afghanistan: The Intelligence Community's Record* (Washington, DC: CIA, April 2002), pp. 13–14. See also Gates, *From the Shadows*, pp. 131–133.
45. *Interagency Intelligence Memorandum: Soviet Options in Afghanistan*, September 28, 1979, p. 1, p. 15, and p. 18.
46. See MacEachin, *Predicting the Soviet Invasion*, pp. 44-47, Gates, *From the Shadows*, pp. 131-133, and "Summary of Conclusions, Special Coordination Committee Meeting" December 17, 1979, in documents assembled for the symposium at Lysebu in 1995, at the National Security Archive in Washington, DC (hereafter Lysebu Binders).
47. CIA, *Soviet Union and Southwest Asia*, January 15, 1980, pp. 1–5.
48. *Interagency Intelligence Memorandum: Soviet Intentions and Options in Southwest Asia: Near-Term Prospects*, March 13, 1980. p. 3.
49. Untitled memorandum quoted in Gates, *From the Shadows*, p. 148.
50. Ibid., p. 148, which provides Turner's paragraph.
51. SNIE 11/34-4-80 *Soviet Military Options in Iran*, August 21, 1980. Iraq invaded Iran on September 22, 1980.
52. Vance, *Hard Choices*, pp. 388–389.
53. Brzezinski, *Power and Principle*, p. 427.

54. "Summary of Conclusions: SCC Meeting on Soviet Moves in Afghanistan," December 26, 1979, in the Lysebu Binders. This document appears to be from Brzezinski to Carter.

55. Memorandum from Brzezinski to Carter, "Reflections on Soviet Intervention in Afghanistan," December 26, 1979. In the original, "regional crisis" is underlined. See also Brzezinski, *Power and Principle*, p. 429. Brzezinski's historical reference to "the age-long dream of Moscow" is problematic. See Raymond L. Garthoff, *Détente and Confrontation: American-Soviet Relations from Nixon to Reagan, Revised Edition* (Washington, DC: Brookings, 1994), p. 1050, fn. 202. Brzezinski's reference to Britain is problematic: the issue was India, not the Indian Ocean. The US can hardly be said to have "replaced" Britain, either in 1945 or afterwards.

56. Memo from Brzezinski to Carter, "Our Response to Soviet Intervention in Afghanistan," December 29, 1979, in the Lysebu Binders.

57. Brzezinski, *Power and Principle*, p. 430.

58. Ibid., p. 431. The date is unclear from the context. For Brzezinski's recommendations, see memorandum from Brzezinski to Carter, "Possible Steps in Reaction to Soviet Intervention in Afghanistan," January 2, 1980, in the Lysebu Binders. See also "Minutes of National Security Council Meeting," January 2, 1980, in the Lysebu Binders.

59. Richard Halloran, "Brown Warns That a Persian Gulf War Could Spread," *New York Times*, February 15, 1980, p. 3.

60. Carter, *Keeping Faith*, pp. 471–472.

61. Publicly, "Text of the President's Address to the Nation," January 4, 1980 and "Talking Points for Telephone Calls on the President's Speech," January 4, 1980. Privately, "Talking Points for Harold Brown Meetings with Chinese Officials in Beijing," January 1980, p. 3, in the Lysebu Binders. Brown was authorized to offer nonlethal military equipment. Brzezinski and Brown wanted to open the door to a US-PRC military relationship (Brzezinski, *Power and Principle*, p. 431), which was opposed by Vance (Vance, *Hard Choices*, pp. 390-391). Carter, decided that it would be a "quantum leap to go to arms sales at this time, It was better, [Carter] concluded, to leave that option open." Brzezinski, p. 431.

62. "State of the Union Address," January 21, 1980.

63. Brzezinski, *Power and Principle*, p. 445.

64. Garthoff, *Détente and Confrontation*, p. 1065.

65. NIE 11-3/8-79 *Soviet Capabilities for Strategic Nuclear Conflict Through the 1980s, Volume 1-Summary*, March 17, 1980, pp. 3–4.

66. NIE 11-3/8-80 *Soviet Capabilities for Strategic Nuclear Conflict Through the Late 1980s*, December 16, 1980, p. A-18.

67. Ibid., pp. B-17 and B-18.

68. Ibid., pp. A-1 through A-19.

69. Garthoff, *Détente and Confrontation*, p. 1083.

70. *Report* (1980), p. 61.

71. *United States Military Posture for FY 1981*, pp. i-ii.

72. PD-62 *Modifications in U.S. National Security Strategy*, January 15, 1981.

73. PD-63 *Persian Gulf Security Framework*, January 15, 1981.

74. "Memorandum to Holders of NIE 11-4-78 *Soviet Expectations in the Global Power Arena*," July 7, 1981, p. 1.

75. NIE 11-4-82 *The Soviet Challenge to US Security Interests*, August 10, 1982, p. 1.

76. NIE 11-3/8-81 *Soviet Capabilities for Strategic Nuclear Conflict, 1981-1991*, March 23, 1982 and NIE 11-3/8-82 *Soviet Capabilities for Strategic Nuclear Conflict, 1982-1992*, February 15, 1983.

77. Raymond L. Garthoff, *The Great Transition: American-Soviet Relations and the End of the Cold War* (Washington, DC: Brookings, 1994), pp. 15–31.

78. Caspar Weinberger, *Fighting for Peace: Seven Critical Years in the Pentagon* (New York: Warner, 1990), p. 34.

79. "National Security Council Meeting," April 16, 1982, p. 6, at Jason Salton-Ebin, "The Reagan Files," www.thereaganfiles.com.

80. Gates, *From the Shadows*, p. 203.

81. Michael Getler, "General Relieved of NSC Job After Unauthorized Speech," *Washington Post*, October 21, 1981, p. A1.

82. NSSD 1-82 *U.S. National Security Strategy*, February 5, 1982.

83. "National Security Council Meeting," April 16, 1982, p. 2, at Jason Salton-Ebin, "The Reagan Files," www.thereaganfiles.com.

84. NSDD-32 *U.S. National Security Strategy*, May 20, 1982, pp. 2–3.

85. NSDD-75 *U.S. Relations with the USSR*, January 17, 1983.

86. *Soviet Strategic Objectives: An Alternative View*, p. 47.

87. "National Security Council Meeting," April 16, 1982, p. 2, at Jason Salton-Ebin, "The Reagan Files," www.thereaganfiles.com.

Chapter Five

Balance of Military Capabilities: Sufficiency of General Purpose Forces

Balance of military capabilities argues that a country balances because it fears that its military forces are insufficient to dissuade another country from attempting to conquer or compel it. Countries can dissuade attempts at conquest and compellence by defense, building forces that an adversary must defeat to enjoy the fruits of conquest, or by deterrence, building forces that can punish an adversary and so make conquest unattractive.

Were US forces sufficient to defend US interests from a Soviet attack or deter the Soviet Union from attacking US interests? Balance of military capabilities would be strengthened as an explanation of US balancing if the US could not have high confidence in its ability to dissuade the Soviet Union, and it would be weakened if the US could be confident in its ability.

The US relied on *general purpose forces*, conventional forces armed with nuclear weapons, to defend US interests from an attack by Soviet general purpose forces, and it relied on *strategic forces*, forces armed with nuclear weapons with intercontinental range, to deter a Soviet attack with either general purpose or strategic forces. This chapter focuses on general purpose forces. The first section considers the quantitative and qualitative growth of Soviet forces in the Brezhnev era and the size of US and Soviet forces. Such aggregations indicate the forces the US and the Soviet Union might draw on in case of conflict, not the forces that would fight each other in specific situations. Actual conflict would occur in geographic regions, or theaters, and it would be the capability to deploy, operate, and sustain forces in particular theaters that would determine military outcomes. The second and third sections assess forces in two theaters, Central Europe and the Persian Gulf. Theaters were not isolated, however, and a war between the US and the Soviet Union might begin in one and spread to others and might eventually lead to nuclear warfare involving the US and Soviet homelands. The fourth section considers the relationship between general purpose forces and nuclear weapons.

STATIC INDICATORS

There was substantial quantitative and qualitative growth of Soviet forces between the mid-1960s and the late 1970s. CIA assessed in 1981 that, since the mid-1960s, the Soviet Union had more than tripled the size of its battlefield nuclear forces and broken NATO's monopoly on nuclear-capable artillery systems and so reduced the credibility of NATO's nuclear weapons as a counterweight to the Warsaw Pact's larger conventional forces. To the extent that Soviet strategic forces checked those of the US and Soviet gains in theater nuclear forces offset those of NATO, the balance of conventional forces had become increasingly important. Soviet forces had improved substantially. The number of major weapons in each Soviet division had increased by about one-third, and artillery firepower had more than doubled. The latest Soviet tanks (common in front-line units in Eastern Europe) had armor that provided good protection against the most advanced antitank weapons though many Soviet units and most Warsaw Pact units were equipped with older, less capable vehicles. The number, variety, and capability of air defense systems had increased rapidly. The Soviet air force had increased nine-fold the weight of ordnance it could deliver deep into NATO territory. The Soviet navy had introduced new surface ships, nuclear powered submarines, and aircraft, and it had quadrupled the number of missile launchers on its ships and submarines. It was a growing constraint on Western ability to project naval power though its forces remained vulnerable to attack by US aircraft and submarines.[1]

Estimates using static indicators showed a substantial and increasing quantitative advantage for the Soviet Union by the mid-1970s. Soviet military personnel had risen from some four million in the mid-1960s to 4.2 million in 1980[2] while US personnel had declined from a peak of over three million in 1968 to about 2.1 million in the mid-1970s. CIA estimated that the number of personnel in the Soviet Ground Forces had risen fifty percent between 1965 and 1980 to 1.7 million.[3] The US Army and US Marine Corps (USMC) together had about one million soldiers. CIA estimated that Soviet forces in 1980 were distributed between 184 divisions and were equipped with 48,000 tanks, 43,000 armored personnel carriers, and 24,000 artillery pieces.[4] Not all Soviet divisions were fully manned and equipped. CIA estimated in 1982 that some eighty-two divisions were able to conduct defensive operations immediately and offensive operations quickly. Some 103 cadre-strength divisions could be filled-out quickly with personnel but would require weeks of training to attain the minimum standard of effectiveness for offensive combat.[5] The US Army had sixteen divisions at varying levels of readiness and was equipped with 10,900 tanks, 22,000 other armored fighting vehicles, and 6500 artillery pieces. The USMC had three large divisions equipped with 575 tanks and 950 amphibious armored fighting vehicles. The US also had eight Army divisions and one USMC division in reserve.[6] The Soviet tactical air force operated some 4800 combat aircraft, an increase of some 1800 since 1965, while the US operated some 3400 combat aircraft, a number that had remained roughly constant since 1970. The Soviet navy operated some 131 major surface combatants and 100 nuclear and 183 diesel attack and cruise missile submarines while the US navy operated about 180 major surface combatants and eighty nuclear attack submarines.[7]

CENTRAL EUROPE

While a war was less likely to originate in Europe than elsewhere, a risk in any US-Soviet confrontation was that it might spread there. Both the US and the Soviet Union had vital interests in Europe, and both had committed much of their military capabilities there, especially to Central Europe.[8] In 1977, CIA estimated that Warsaw Pact forces in Central Europe operated 18,600 tanks, 5800 artillery pieces, and 2800 major antitank weapons while NATO forces in the region (including France) operated 9200 tanks, 3000 artillery pieces, and 5600 major antitank weapons.[9] According to the Office of the Secretary of Defense/Program Analysis and Evaluation (OSD/PA&E), the Warsaw Pact in 1978 deployed eighty-nine divisions for operations in Central Europe comprised of twenty-seven Soviet divisions in Eastern Europe, thirty-one East German, Czechoslovak, and Polish divisions, twenty-eight Soviet divisions in the western Soviet Union, and three airborne divisions. These forces could be fully mobilized and in the theater by fifteen days after mobilization (M+15). The Soviet Union might commit an additional nineteen divisions from its strategic reserve.[10] NATO deployed 34.3 division equivalents, including two US armored divisions, two US mechanized infantry divisions, and five French divisions. In 1978, the US planned to deploy an additional 12.3 divisions by M+60; that number was projected to increase to eighteen by 1984. In terms of Armored Division Equivalents (ADEs), which compares disparate kinds of divisions with a US armored division,[11] the Warsaw Pact in 1978 deployed about 70.64 ADEs for operations in Central Europe, of which twenty-seven were in Soviet forces in Eastern Europe, 23.34 were in Soviet forces in the western Soviet Union, and 20.3 were in Polish, Czechoslovak, and East German forces.[12] NATO deployed about 30.55 ADEs in the region. The US expected to deploy about 8.5 additional ADEs by M+30 in 1978.[13]

A number of factors had altered the balance to NATO's disadvantage over the preceding years including modernization and augmentation of Soviet conventional forces, continued Soviet commitment to improving the Warsaw Pact's capability, and the quantitative and qualitative growth of Soviet tactical nuclear forces. Warsaw Pact capability had increased after 1968 when the Soviet Union stationed five divisions in Czechoslovakia and began increasing the number of personnel and armored vehicles in its divisions. The quality of the equipment had improved, especially in tanks and air defense forces, and the Soviet army introduced the BMP mechanized infantry combat vehicle in the mid-1960s and self-propelled artillery in the mid-1970s. The Warsaw Pact air forces in the region had been transformed from a short-range interceptor force poorly capable of close air support and interdiction to a balanced force capable of attacks throughout Central Europe. CIA estimated that the Soviet leadership believed that Soviet theater nuclear forces reduced the political and military utility of such weapons to NATO and that Soviet acquisition of nuclear-capable artillery would reduce the deterrent value of such systems for NATO because the Soviet Union could retaliate without escalation. The credibility of NATO's nuclear forces as a counter to larger Warsaw Pact conventional forces had eroded, and the basis of deterrence in Europe was likely to shift to conventional forces. However, increasing Soviet confidence was likely to be tempered by an awareness of projected improvements in NATO capability and the possibility that NATO could generate new systems that would open new areas of competition.[14]

While the quantity of Warsaw Pact forces was expected to remain about the same into the mid-1980s, the quality of those forces was expected to improve. By 1984, Soviet forces in Central Europe were expected to increase from twenty-seven ADEs to thirty-one, Soviet forces in the western Soviet Union were expected to increase from 23.4 ADEs to twenty-nine, and German, Polish, and Czechoslovak forces were expected to increase from 20.3 to 23.8 ADEs so total Warsaw Pact ADEs would increase from about seventy-one in 1978 to almost eighty-four in 1984, an increase of over eighteen percent.[15] NATO improvements, if fully implemented, were expected to increase in-place ADEs about nineteen percent from 30.55 in 1978 to 36.4 in 1984. In addition, the rate at which US reinforcements would arrive was increasing so the Warsaw Pact advantage would be reduced to about 1.9:1 ADEs through M+30 and then down to 1.6:1 thereafter.[16]

Warsaw Pact forces were likely to mobilize quickly so lags in initiation and execution of NATO mobilization would hurt NATO. Warsaw Pact strength would be close to its peak about M+14 while NATO strength would increase rapidly through M+14, increase slowly through M+21, and would then increase substantially after M+30.[17] OSD/PA&E projected that, in 1984, the Warsaw Pact might have 41.3 ADEs on M+4 while NATO might have twenty-eight.[18] OSD/PA&E judged that NATO forces would be sufficient for an initial defense of a static front but reserves of one British and one German division in the Northern Army Group (NORTHAG) and one German and five French divisions in the Central Army Group were insufficient in the absence of US reinforcements. Warsaw Pact forces might have 78.74 ADEs on M+15 while NATO, assuming a five-day mobilization lag, would have 39.45. The Warsaw Pact could concentrate its forces and so translate its 2:1 theater advantage to a 6:1 local advantage which would have a good chance of breaking through the front. Such conditions would require skillful employment of reserves to maintain a defense. NATO prospects improved as US reinforcements arrived. The US would provide reinforcements equal to 5.79 ADEs by M+15, an additional 1.64 ADEs by M+30, and another twelve ADEs between M+30 and M+60.[19]

How quickly might the Warsaw Pact commence operations? There was considerable concern in the mid-1970s that NATO might receive little warning of a Soviet attack, perhaps forty-eight hours (D-day = M+2), and there was some concern later that the Soviet Union might initiate hostilities from a "standing start" (D-day = M-day).[20] However, Soviet dependence on Non-Soviet Warsaw Pact (NSWP) forces in such an attack and the increase in capability as forces arrived from the western Soviet Union that was more rapid than the increase in NATO capability gave the Soviet Union incentives not to launch an attack from a standing start. Assuming NATO mobilization quickly followed Warsaw Pact mobilization, Warsaw Pact force ratios were highest after initial mobilization and increasingly worse as US reinforcements arrived. The intelligence community estimated that, except in extraordinarily urgent circumstances, the Warsaw Pact would prefer to reinforce its forces in Central Europe and that there was virtually no chance that Soviet forces would attack from a standing start.[21]

For NATO, the questions were how long the lag would be between Warsaw Pact and NATO M-day, and whether mobilization would be homogeneous or heterogeneous. CIA was confident that it could detect Soviet mobilization early in the process, within hours in the extremely unlikely event of an unprovoked attack from a peacetime posture and by M+1 for larger-scale attacks, because of the intelligence community's "ability to monitor, in near real-time, the normal pattern of Soviet and East European military and civilian activity in peacetime."[22] While Warsaw Pact mobilization activities might be observed, there would likely be different interpretations of what observations meant and how NATO should respond. Initiation of the shift from national to NATO command of forces was a political process that varied from government to government and might take different lengths of time. A decision by Belgium or the Netherlands not to participate would have created a hole in northern Germany; while it would have been filled, it would stretch the defenses in that area. OSD/PA&E estimated that unavailability of some Dutch, British, Belgian, and German units in NORTHAG for a Warsaw Pact attack with forty divisions on M+4 in 1984 might reduce NATO from 11.8 ADEs to 8.8 ADEs so the Warsaw Pact/NATO ratio there might change from 1.49:1 to 2.1:1. OSD/PA&E estimated that this would increase the ability of the Warsaw Pact to gain ground but would not allow it to gain a rapid, decisive breakthrough.[23]

Mobilization was likely to be a difficult process even with political will. The US conducted a large-scale command post exercise involving senior civilian and military officials, NIFTY NUGGET, in 1978 simulating the transportation of 400,000 troops and 350,000 tons of supplies across the Atlantic over a three week period following months of political warning and one week between the president's declaration of an emergency and the initiation of hostilities in Europe. The tightly planned mobilization process devolved into chaos. There were some improvements in US mobilization capability, but another exercise in 1980, PROUD SPIRIT, encountered similar difficulties.[24]

In sum, NATO had a reasonable chance of defending the territory of its members in Central Europe if the Warsaw Pact launched a short-warning attack with in-place forces and US reinforcements arrived as scheduled. They also had a reasonable chance if NATO had more than thirty days of mobilization and mobilization worked as expected. The Soviet Union was unlikely to launch a short-warning attack because of the difficulties of coordinating Warsaw Pact forces and because Warsaw Pact prospects were better if it mobilized more fully. A long-warning attack was plausible because an attack might be preceded by an extended crisis, though, recognizing that time was on NATO's side, the Soviet Union might choose to attack before NATO finished mobilizing. However, NATO prospects were critically dependent on mobilization of NATO forces and arrival of US reinforcements, and delays or failures in either would have decreased NATO's ability to defend Central Europe against either a short- or long-warning attack.

NATO could not have high confidence of defending against a Warsaw Pact attack in the period between M+15, when the Warsaw Pact's eighty-nine divisions and almost eighty ADEs would be fully mobilized while NATO would have fewer than forty ADEs, and the deployment of large US forces, which would begin on NATO M+30. The US was concerned about the ability of NATO forces in this period and sought to remedy these deficiencies.

There is a danger that this analysis overstates NATO vulnerability because it does not consider problems that the Warsaw Pact might face. Mobilization might not be a smooth process for the Warsaw Pact because it was composed of semi-sovereign countries with varying levels of commitment whose forces would be conducting offensive operations outside of their territories. Until 1979, Warsaw Pact forces were commanded as national forces in peacetime and would have been assigned to a Soviet-dominated command structure for wartime operations. This was not an automatic process and would take time.[25] This changed in 1979 when the Soviet Union gained the authority to transfer NSWP forces to Soviet command.[26] However, NSWP countries might still attempt to avoid participation in Soviet offensive operations. Open source and classified estimates assessed that East Germany was likely to be a reliable participant but that Czechoslovakia was questionable. There was a range of estimates about Poland; if Polish forces entered the war, they might have been reliable in initial operations and might have remained so if initial operations were successful.[27] Warsaw Pact logistics would also be problematic.[28] Finally, this analysis does not consider command and control, which would be challenging for both sides. The focus on NATO deficiencies is legitimate because I am assessing causes of US balancing behavior, and the US could not assume that the Warsaw Pact would necessarily encounter these problems.

SOUTHWEST ASIA

The Soviet Union deployed forces on its own territory capable of invading Iran and so threatening Western access to Persian Gulf oil, a vital US interest. In 1979, the Soviet Union deployed two airborne divisions and fifteen low readiness motorized rifle divisions with older equipment as well as about 400 tactical combat aircraft in the two military districts adjacent to Iran.[29] There were five more motorized rifle divisions and one tank division, all at low readiness, in the North Caucasus Military District.[30] SNIE 11/39-4-80 estimated in 1980 that the Soviet Union would prefer to use sixteen to twenty divisions in a large invasion of Iran; its preparations might take one month though it would probably prefer to take several months to ready its forces. However, it could launch a hasty attack aimed at seizing major objectives in Iran, including some on the Persian Gulf coast, with ten to twelve ill-prepared divisions within two weeks.[31] Soviet forces could be readily reinforced, albeit at the cost of reducing reserves available for European and East Asian contingencies. Additional forces would allow the Soviet Union to occupy the western littoral of the Persian Gulf from Kuwait to Oman. In 1983, NIE 11/39-83 D estimated that, "in the absence of a Western response," such an operation might require an additional ten to fifteen divisions.[32] Soviet intervention in Afghanistan in December 1979 placed Soviet forces closer to the Persian Gulf and would have allowed an invasion of Iran from the east as well as the north. However, a Soviet assault on the Persian Gulf through Iran would face serious difficulties. It is over 600 straight-line miles from the Soviet-Iranian border on either side of the Caspian Sea to the northern edge of the Persian Gulf. The road network is sparse, and it runs through extensive mountainous areas. It is about 300 straight-line miles from where the Afghan-Iran-Pakistan borders meet to the Straits of Hormuz and an additional 100 miles to where a significant road enters Iran from Afghanistan. The road network is poorly developed and traverses several mountain ranges. It would take Soviet forces time to traverse such routes unopposed, and even light opposition in the mountainous areas would impose substantial delays. It would be difficult to support Soviet forces logistically, probably requiring the logistical assets of many divisions to support a small number conducting operations.

Where the Soviet Union could deploy large forces on its own territory near the Persian Gulf and could invade Iran from the Soviet Union and, after 1979, from Afghanistan, the US was poorly positioned to defend its interests in the region. The US did not operate ground or air forces in the region, and navy forces in the area would take time to reinforce. Logistics for all services were likely to be problematic because of the distances involved. According to Secretary of Defense Harold Brown, the US could quickly airlift a "lightly armed" brigade but the movement of a mechanized or armored brigade would engage most of the US airlift capacity for some time, even assuming that basing and overflight rights were available.[33] Using all airlift capability plus civilian aircraft, it might take almost four weeks to move both the 82nd and 101st divisions to the Persian Gulf; it might take about five weeks to move a heavy division and either of the two aforementioned light divisions to the region.[34]

Concern about US capability to intervene in the Persian Gulf had been voiced in 1977 in PRM-10, the national security study conducted by the incoming Carter administration, and the resultant national strategy directive, PD-18, had directed that the US would be able to deploy military forces, independent of local bases and support, able to fight both local and Soviet forces in the Middle East, the Persian Gulf, or Korea.[35] The situation was improving as the US acquired greater airlift capacity and fourteen Maritime Prepositioning Ships and the equipment for three Marine brigades over five years.[36] As an intermediate step, seven ships with sufficient equipment and supplies for a Marine brigade and several Air Force squadrons were deployed in the Indian Ocean in July 1980. In addition, the US established the Joint Rapid Deployment Task Force (JRDTF) to command forces in the region though no forces were assigned to it.

The Reagan administration was also concerned about the ability of the US to defend its interests in the Persian Gulf. The first of two NSC meetings about NSSD 1-82, the review of US strategy, focused on the region. The participants spoke of the need for seven additional divisions plus support if the area was to be defended. Secretary of Defense Caspar Weinberger also emphasized the need for additional transportation capability and "the full cooperation of regional states."[37]

GENERAL PURPOSE FORCES AND NUCLEAR WEAPONS

Overshadowing any military interaction between the US and the Soviet Union was the possibility that nuclear weapons might be used. Fundamental NATO strategy articulated in 1968 in MC 14/3 *Overall Strategic Concept for the Defense of the North Atlantic Treaty Organization Area* specified a forward "Direct Defence" with conventional forces supplemented by the capability to employ nuclear weapons within the theater plus the capability necessary for "Deliberate Escalation." The ultimate deterrent and the ultimate military action was "General Nuclear Response." Moreover, MC 14/3 specified that 'the strategic nuclear forces of the Alliance should be adequate to inflict catastrophic damage on Soviet society even after a surprise nuclear attack' and "constitute the backbone of NATO's military capabilities."[38] Similarly, nuclear weapons might be employed in any conflict between the US and Soviet Union outside Europe. While MC 14/3 specified escalation from conventional warfare to employment of nuclear weapons within Europe and then against the Soviet homeland, the threat logically implicit in any use of nuclear weapons, in Europe or elsewhere, was that they might be used without regard to the military situation and conflict might involve intercontinental weapons without the nominally intermediate stage of tactical nuclear weapons. Hence, the price paid by the Soviet Union might be much greater than any conceivable gain from conventional operations and was independent of the success of those operations.

What effect would employment of nuclear weapons have on the course of warfare? When they are unlikely to be used, conventional forces can concentrate for offensive, defensive, and counteroffensive operations. When their use is possible, concentrated forces become likely targets so units would probably disperse in a "nuclear-scared" posture and forces would probably "hug" their enemy so that nuclear weapons could not be employed without damaging the user's forces. Forces conducting offensive operations would move rapidly and concentrate at a late stage. Forces on the defensive would also be dispersed, making it easier for offensive forces that successfully concentrate to penetrate the front. Movement might make it difficult to target troop formations, and targeting would be even more difficult when forces are intermingled. In addition, command and control, already nightmarish given the pace of operations, will, depending to some extent on the scale and character of employment, become even more difficult in a nuclear environment and more likely to break down. To the extent that the US believed that NATO could conduct a more coherent, and so effective, defense and the Soviet Union believed that the Warsaw Pact could conduct a more coherent, and so effective, offense, both sides had incentives to avoid employing nuclear weapons.[39]

Increasing recognition of the problems associated with theater nuclear weapons led to an evolution in expectations about their role. Where the US military envisioned an essentially nuclear battlefield in Europe in the 1950s in part to offset perceived Soviet conventional superiority, MC 14/3 stated that NATO would attempt to defend Europe with conventional forces before escalating to nuclear weapons employment in Europe and then directly against the Soviet Union. Soviet doctrine and expectations evolved through several phases. Between 1960 and 1965, nuclear weapons were seen as revolutionary and diminishing the role of conventional forces. Soviet planning expected to attack the US preemptively and to follow up with an offensive against Western Europe involving preemptive nuclear strikes followed by a conventional offensive lasting about ten days.[40] Between 1965 and 1975, war in Europe was still expected to be nuclear though it might start with a conventional phase that in the mid-1960s was expected to last for hours and in the mid-1970s was expected to last for up to a week. NATO was expected to initiate use of nuclear weapons; the Soviet Union was likely to respond in kind within the theater but was unlikely to escalate to intercontinental attacks. By the late 1970s, the General Staff foresaw the possibility that the conventional phase might be long, and by the early 1980s that a war might remain conventional in part because SS-20 IRBMs were expected to deter use of nuclear weapons by NATO.[41] NIE 11-14-79 stated that the Soviet leadership expected that the initial stages of a NATO-Warsaw Pact conflict would probably be fought with conventional forces but that NATO was likely to use nuclear weapons to avoid defeat and the Soviet Union was likely to use them if the war was going badly for the Warsaw Pact.[42]

The net effect of this evolution of expectations about nuclear weapons was both a reduced likelihood of war for fear of the consequences of use and escalation, and an increased emphasis on conventional forces for both the US and the Soviet Union. The Soviet Union could not assume that the US would not employ nuclear weapons if it faced defeat in Europe or the Persian Gulf but the US could not assume that its nuclear capability offset Soviet conventional superiority and so remedied the balance of military capabilities problem faced by the US.

CONCLUSIONS

Soviet forces had more personnel and major weapons systems than US forces, Warsaw Pact forces had more weapons systems than NATO, and the quality of Warsaw Pact forces was improving. The US could have confidence in the ability of NATO to defend Europe only in the particular circumstances of a short-warning attack before the Warsaw Pact was fully mobilized or after US reinforcements arrived in Europe. The US could not have high confidence in the ability of NATO to defend Europe in the period between when the Warsaw Pact was largely mobilized and US reinforcements arrived or if NATO mobilization lagged Warsaw Pact mobilization. NATO was critically dependent on US reinforcements, and delays in their arrival would appreciably weaken NATO defenses in all cases. Increasing Warsaw Pact capabilities meant the distribution of military capabilities would continue to move against the US unless the US and NATO increased their own capabilities.

The US situation worsened in 1979 when the Iranian Revolution in February removed the keystone US ally which would have provided a friendly reception to US forces. The introduction of Soviet forces into Afghanistan in December apparently improved Soviet ability to introduce forces into the Persian Gulf region. The US was poorly positioned to defend its interests in the Persian Gulf and faced requirements for additional capabilities after 1979 to have confidence that it could defend its interests.

The increasing difficulties of defending Central Europe and the Persian Gulf argue in favor of a balance of military capabilities explanation, which expects to find that US forces were insufficient in at least one theater and finds they were insufficient in two.

NOTES

1. CIA, *The Development of Soviet Military Power: Trends Since 1965 and Prospects for the 1980s*, April 1, 1981, pp. iii–xv.
2. Ibid., p. 38.
3. Ibid., p. 14. See chapter 2 for a discussion of total military personnel.
4. Ibid., p. 3.
5. CIA, *The Readiness of Soviet Ground Forces*, November 1, 1982, pp. 1–2. See also CIA, DIA, and US Army, *Soviet Ground Forces Trends*, October 1984, p. iii.

6. US Army National Guard infantry divisions might be deployed six weeks after being mobilized though they would require an additional four weeks to be fully ready for combat. Armored and mechanized divisions might attain minimal combat capability in nine to ten weeks, though tank gunners and signals personnel would not attain proficiency until four months after mobilization. John M. Collins, *American and Soviet Military Trends Since the Cuban Missile Crisis* (Washington, DC: Center for Strategic and International Studies, 1978), p. 180.

7. Data for Soviet forces are from CIA, *The Development of Soviet Military Power*, p. 3. Data for US forces are from International Institute for Strategic Studies (hereafter IISS), *The Military Balance, 1979-1980* (London: IISS, 1979), pp. 5–11 and *Report of Secretary of Defense Harold Brown to the Congress on the FY 1980 Budget, FY 1981 Authorization Request and FY 1980-1984 Defense Programs, January 25, 1979*, pp. 88–91 (hereafter *Report* (year)).

8. Central Europe is defined as Belgium, Czechoslovakia, Denmark, the Federal Republic of Germany, the German Democratic Republic, the Netherlands, and Poland.

9. CIA, *The Balance of Forces in Central Europe*, August 1977, p. 6.

10. Office of the Secretary of Defense/Program Analysis and Evaluation (hereafter OSD/PA&E), *NATO Center Region Balance Study, 1978–1984*, July 13, 1979, p. I–6.

11. ADE is a measure of combat power that includes quantity and quality of weapons and which takes into account firepower, survivability, and mobility.

12. OSD/PA&E, *NATO Center Region Balance Study*, p. I–7. Note that this shows the average Soviet division in Eastern Europe as equivalent to one US armored division.

13. Ibid., p. I–17. Note that this shows the average NATO division as equivalent to .89 of a US armored division.

14. CIA, *The Balance of Nuclear Forces in Central Europe*, January 1, 1978, pp. i–ii.

15. OSD/PA&E, *NATO Center Region Balance Study*, p. I–7.

16. Ibid., p. 6 and p. I–12.

17. CIA, *Balance of Forces in Central Europe*, pp. 8-10. See also NIE 4-1-78 *Warsaw Pact Concepts and Capabilities for Going to War in Europe: Implications for NATO Warning of War*, April 10, 1978, p. 12; CIA, *The Readiness of Soviet Ground Forces*, p. 24; Robert Lucas Fischer, *Defending the Central Front: The Balance of Forces*, Adelphi Paper 127 (London: IISS, 1976), p. 23; and Richard K. Betts, *Surprise Attack* (Washington, DC: Brookings, 1982), pp. 181–184.

18. OSD/PA&E, *NATO Center Region Balance Study*, p. I–29.

19. Ibid., p. I–33 and p. I–34.

20. See, for example, Senate Armed Services Committee, *NATO and the New Soviet Threat: Report of Sen. Sam Nunn and Sen. Dewey F. Bartlett* (Washington, DC: US GPO, January 24, 1977). See Rep. Les Aspin, *Congressional Record — House*, February 7, 1977, pp. 3813–3816 for an argument that such an attack was improbable. See also Betts, *Surprise Attack*, pp. 180–181.

21. NIE 4-1-78, p. 12 and NIE 11-14-79 *Warsaw Pact Forces Opposite NATO*, January 31, 1979, pp. 7–9, pp. 12–13, and p. 53, NARA RG 263, E 29, Box 17. See

also NIE 11-14-81 *Warsaw Pact Forces Opposite NATO*, July 7, 1981; and CIA, *Warning of War in Europe*, June 27, 1984.

22. NIE 4-1-78, p. 3 and pp. 39–40.

23. OSD/PA&E, *NATO Center Region Balance Study*, p. I-29 and p. I-30.

24. Michael Getler, "Make-Believe Mobilization Showed Major Flaws," *Washington Post*, July 24, 1980, p. A6, Betts; *Surprise Attack*, pp. 185-186; and Thomas B. Allen, *War Games* (New York: McGraw-Hill, 1987), pp. 255–265.

25. NIE 11-14-79 estimated about a week. NIE 11-14-79, p. 49.

26. See "Statute of the United Command in War Time," March 18, 1980 in Vojtech Mastny and Malcolm Byrne, *A Cardboard Castle? An Inside History of the Warsaw Pact, 1955–1991* (New York: Central European University Press, 2005), pp. 427–434 and NIE 12/11-83 *Military Reliability of the Soviet Union's Warsaw Pact Allies*, June 28, 1983, p. 10 and pp. 25–26.

27. CIA, *The Balance of Forces in Central Europe*, pp. 6–8; Dale R. Herspring and Ivan Volgyes, "How Reliable are Eastern European Armies," *Survival* 22, no. 5 (September/October 1980); A. Ross Johnson, Robert W. Dean, and Alexander Alexiev, "The Armies of the Warsaw Pact Northern Tier," *Survival* 23, no. 4 (July/August 1981); and NIE 12/11-83, p. 5.

28. For example, the rail network in eastern Poland was sparse and used a different gauge than the Soviet network. Soviet cargoes would arrive at one of about eight facilities on the Polish/Soviet border where cargo and personnel would either be transloaded or the wheels switched. The Polish rail system might accommodate movement of two divisions per day, moving twenty trains on each of seven lines each day. The highway network in eastern Poland was also sparse. See Office of Technology Assessment, *New Technology for NATO: Implementing Follow-On Forces Attack* (Washington, DC: US GPO, 1987). Soviet forces began augmenting stockpiles in Eastern Europe in the mid-1970s; by 1987, CIA estimated that stockpiles would "support combat operations of a force twice as large as that now in place for 60 to 90 days. CIA, *Readiness of Soviet Forces in Central Europe*, p. v.

29. CIA, "Memorandum: Soviet Forces in the Transcaucasus and Turkestan Military Districts," November 23, 1979.

30. SNIE 11/34-4-80 *Soviet Military Options in Iran*, August 21, 1980, pp. 9–10.

31. Ibid., p. 2.

32. NIE 11/39-83 D *Soviet Forces and Capabilities in the Southern Theater of Military Operations*, December 1983, p. 10.

33. *Report* (1980), pp. 116–117.

34. Congressional Budget Office, *U.S. Airlift Forces: Enhancement Alternatives for NATO and Non-NATO Contingencies* (Washington, DC: US GPO, 1979), p. 56.

35. Re. PRM-10, see Zbigniew Brzezinski, *Power and Principle: Memoirs of the National Security Adviser, 1977–1981* (New York: Farrar, Straus and Giroux, 1983), p. 177. PD-18 *U.S. National Strategy*, August 24, 1977, p. 4.

36. *Report* (1980), pp. 116–117.

37. "National Security Council Meeting," April 16, 1982, at Jason Salton-Ebin, "The Reagan Files," www.thereaganfiles.com.

38. North Atlantic Military Committee, MC 14/3 (Final), *Overall Strategic Concept for the Defense of the North Atlantic Treaty Organization Area*, January 16, 1968, in Gregory W. Pedlow, ed., *NATO Strategy Documents, 1949–1969*, www.nato.int/archives/strategy.htm. MC 14/3 was not replaced until 1991.

39. Both sides, though, might launch conventional attacks against nuclear systems, though this might cause inadvertent escalation.

40. John G. Hines, Ellis M. Mishulovich, and John Shull, *Soviet Intentions 1965–1985. Volume I: An Analytical Comparison of U.S.-Soviet Assessments During the Cold War* (McLean, VA: BDM, September 22, 1995), pp. 72–76. See also Stephen M. Meyer, *Soviet Theatre Nuclear Forces, Part I: Development of Doctrine and Objectives*, Adelphi Paper 187 (London: IISS, 1983/1984) and *Soviet Theatre Nuclear Forces, Part II: Capabilities and Implications*, Adelphi Paper 188, Ibid., and David M. Glantz, *Soviet Military Operational Art: In Pursuit of Deep Battle* (London: Frank Cass, 1991), pp. 177–244.

41. Regarding a conventional period and the possibility of a purely conventional war, see Ghulam Dastagir Wardak, *The Voroshilov Lectures: Materials from the Soviet General Staff Academy, Volume I: Issues of Military Strategy*, ed. Graham Hall Turbiville, Jr. (Washington, DC: National Defense University Press, 1989), pp. 72–75 and pp. 244–255.

42. NIE 11-14-79, p. 1 and p. 22.

Chapter Six

Balance of Military Capabilities: US Wartime Prospects

A second observable implication of balance of military capabilities is about the perceptions of a country's leadership of its prospects in war. Balance of military capabilities expects that the US leadership was not confident that the US had good prospects in a war with the Soviet Union and generated military capabilities to improve them. Balance of military capabilities will be weakened if the US leadership was confident that the US had good prospects in a war with the Soviet Union. How did the US leadership perceive US prospects in the mid-1970s and early 1980s? The first section considers assessments prepared by the late Ford and early Carter administrations and statements by their secretaries of defense. This section includes the most significant evidence, the explicit assessments of likely war outcomes in the PRM-10 military strategy and force posture study. The second section considers statements by Secretary of Defense Harold Brown, a study about the balance of forces in Central Europe, and national security statements prepared by President Jimmy Carter's NSC in 1981 and President Ronald Reagan's NSC in 1982.

1976–1977

The Ford and Carter administrations conducted reviews of the distribution of military capabilities in late 1976 and early 1977. NSSM-246, signed by President Gerald Ford in September 1976, requested an assessment of the distribution of military capabilities.[1] The resulting study was discussed at a NSC meeting on December 15. The participants were concerned about the long-term Soviet military buildup and assessed it as the primary national security problem that the US would face over the next decade. The meeting concluded with Ford indicating his preference for moderately improved intercontinental forces with better counter-silo capability; additional combat aircraft; improved sustainability in Europe and flexibility with respect to warning time; and increased worldwide capability, including airlift.[2] Where the consensus of the meeting was that Soviet strategic and general purpose forces posed a substantial problem for the US, the picture that emerges from the resulting NSDM-348 *U.S. Defense Policy and Military Posture* is one in which the US was not particularly challenged by Soviet military capability. US ICBM silos were vulnerable but the triad was robust and provided an assured second strike capable of both a massive counter-recovery attack and smaller, flexible responses. Increasingly capable Warsaw Pact forces "could be met with appropriate modernization and posture adjustments by the U.S. and its NATO allies" though NATO's flanks and sustainability were problematic. The US would require suitable forces for likely challenges outside of Europe. Where the NSC meeting had at least mentioned Japan, Korea, and the Middle East, NSDM-348 was a Euro-centric document with only passing reference to generic non-NATO contingencies.[3]

The new Carter administration's PRM-10 commissioned two studies, a "broadly gauged review of the US-Soviet strategic balance" led by Samuel Huntington and a military posture review.[4] The first was a "dynamic net assessment" reviewing and comparing the overall trends in political, diplomatic, economic, technological, and military capabilities of the US, its allies, and potential adversaries. It assessed the Soviet Union as making great strides in military capabilities. It was apprehensive about the ability of NATO to withstand a Soviet attack in Europe, and it was concerned about the vulnerability of the Persian Gulf region and the ability of US forces to protect it. The US needed to increase the capabilities of its general purpose and intercontinental nuclear forces. The report was confident, however, about the overall ability of the US to compete politically, economically, and ideologically with the Soviet Union.[5]

The military posture review estimated the outcome of a war between the US and the Soviet Union. It assessed the chance of NATO stopping a Warsaw Pact attack with minimal loss of territory and then regaining lost territory as remote but considered it unlikely that the Warsaw Pact would achieve its full objective of defeating NATO forces in Central Europe and reaching the French border and the North Sea coast. NATO's flanks could probably be defended with some loss of territory if a defensive line could be established in Central Europe. Soviet naval forces attempting to interdict NATO supply lines in the Atlantic were likely to experience significant attrition, and NATO was likely to attain eventual control over the Mediterranean. The ability of the US and its allies to prevail against the Soviet Union outside of Europe in a general war was uncertain. Neither side could conceivably be characterized as a "winner" in a major nuclear exchange regardless of which side was the initiator and regardless of warning. In Asia, the US had the maritime advantage of control of choke points, access to bases, and the opportunity to attack targets in Soviet territory. Essential shipping to Japan could probably be maintained, though economic and lines of communication might not and so might endanger Japan's continued support of US military operations. Major uncertainties included the effectiveness of Soviet attempts to interrupt the flow of oil from the Middle East; actions by China, North Korea, and Vietnam; and Japanese resilience. Concerning limited war contingencies, the US was likely to prevail if it fought the Soviet Union in the Middle East, the US had a substantial advantage in sub-Saharan Africa, and the US and South Korea would prevail after initial North Korean successes in Korea.[6]

The review did not assess the situation in Southwest Asia, especially the possibility of a Soviet attempt to gain control over the Persian Gulf that was to be of such concern within a few years. Rather, the report explicitly assumed that NATO would depend on existing oil stockpiles until forces could be freed from other theaters. Written after the 1973 oil crisis, there was an awareness of energy issues but not the sense that the Persian Gulf was a vital interest for the US and a place where war might begin. In addition, there was likely an assumption that Iran could be relied upon as an ally able to defend the Persian Gulf from the Soviet Union and a host country for US forces defending the region.[7]

The PRM-10 studies led to PD-18 *U.S. National Strategy*, which articulated US military goals as counterbalancing Soviet military power and influence in Europe, the Middle East, and East Asia by military forces, political efforts, and economic programs in concert with US allies. The US would "maintain an overall balance of military power between the United States and its allies on the one hand and the Soviet Union and its allies on the other at least as favorable as that that now exists" and the US would increase real defense spending approximately three percent each year.[8] The US would maintain "essential equivalence" with the Soviet Union in strategic forces. The NATO strategy of "forward defense" was reaffirmed.[9] According to a contemporary account, US forces were intended to be strong enough to deter a Soviet attack and to end a war on the most favorable terms possible to the US. In Europe, the US would enhance the capability of US forces to meet an attack launched with little warning and improve the sustainability of US forces.[10] PD-18 also specified that the US would maintain general purpose forces that could be deployed independent of access to local bases and logistical support that were designed for use against both local forces and forces that the Soviet Union might project. The US would withdraw forces from Korea but would otherwise maintain existing forces in East Asia.[11]

With respect to Europe, both the Ford and Carter administrations publicly assessed that a Warsaw Pact offensive could seize significant NATO territory but probably would not achieve its full objective of defeating NATO. Secretary of Defense Donald Rumsfeld stated in the annual report to the Congress in January 1977 that the US and NATO had sufficient forces to defend Europe, even with short warning. However, he was not confident of conducting a successful forward defense in all situations, and, without prompt remedial action, NATO might lack adequate mobility and firepower.[12] The next month, Brown stated that:

> ... [NATO's] comparative advantages are waning, and the conventional balance in Europe—while not badly tilted against NATO—is more precarious than it should be. While the Pact cannot be confident of breaking through NATO's forward defenses, NATO cannot be confident of preventing a major breakthrough.
>
> We and our allies need to do more to make the odds less unfavorable and to minimize the risks of intimidation in a crisis. However, our problems seem to be less a shortage of forces than they are such remediable weaknesses of the current forces as maldeployment, inadequate readiness, too few artillery tubes and insufficient long-range wide-bodied aircraft modified to handle oversized cargoes.[13]

Both the Ford and Carter administrations were concerned about the growth of Soviet military capability. Neither was confident about the ability of NATO to defend Europe against a Soviet attack though neither expected a Soviet attack to attain its full goals. Both assessed readiness and sustainability as critical deficiencies. While the discussion of the NSSM-246 study had given some consideration to the Middle East and Asia, NSDM-348 was a Euro-centric document that emphasized the possibility that the Soviet Union might attack NATO. While the PRM-10 studies and PD-18 recognized this possibility, they differed by emphasizing extra-European contingencies, especially the possibility that the US might desire to project forces into the Persian Gulf region.

1979–1982

There was greater concern about US prospects a few years later. In 1979, Brown acknowledged a "widespread opinion that the Warsaw Pact could rapidly overcome NATO's defenses regardless of when or how the attack started." He argued that NATO had already acquired most of the basic capabilities necessary to conduct a successful forward defense though he also observed that the Warsaw Pact had expanded and upgraded its forces. "The result of these actions by the two sides is an ambiguous situation. Even today, the Soviets cannot be confident of a rapid conventional victory in Europe. But NATO . . . cannot have as much confidence in its non-nuclear deterrent as I consider prudent."[14] In 1980, Brown stated that NATO would be much more nearly in balance with the Warsaw Pact in the following years so long as the allies proceeded with planned modernization of their forces and US continued its program to deploy forces rapidly to reinforce Europe.

> However, even with these improvements, NATO will not have as high a level of confidence as I would like of containing a large attack by the Pact launched with little preparation and warning. I should add that the Soviets could not have high confidence of a breakthrough either — on the assumption that U.S. reinforcements would arrive on time and could sustain themselves adequately in combat.[15]

The JCS stated in 1980 that "Over the past decade, the balance of conventional forces in Europe and at sea has been moving against the United States and its NATO allies." The US maintained a modest margin of superiority in the Atlantic and the balance in the Mediterranean continued to favor NATO.[16] According to the Joint Chiefs of Staff (JCS), only two conclusions about a NATO-Warsaw Pact conflict seemed warranted: the Warsaw Pact could not be confident that it could achieve a quick victory in Europe and NATO could not be entirely confident that it could successfully defend Europe without using nuclear weapons.[17]

The 1979 OSD/PA&E *NATO Center Region Military Balance Study 1978-1984*, which involved a number of senior Defense Department officials, assessed likely outcomes of three scenarios for a war in Central Europe set in 1984. Its conclusions were similar to those of PRM-10 and consonant with public statements by Brown and others that the Warsaw Pact could not be confident of victory but that NATO could not be confident about successfully defending Central Europe. The study assessed a Warsaw Pact attack with forty divisions four days after Warsaw Pact mobilization (M+4) as risky for the Warsaw Pact. It was likely to make some territorial gains but major gains were unlikely. The Warsaw Pact was likely to make greater territorial gains if some Dutch, British, Belgian, and German units did not deploy in a timely manner, but even then Warsaw Pact forces were unlikely to achieve a decisive breakthrough. NATO would have greater difficulties if its forces failed "to be ready with short warning" and it faced "the vulnerabilities arising from inadequately-prepared defenses, and the difficulty in promptly maneuvering forces into place in such a fluid situation."[18] The study also considered a Warsaw Pact attack with eighty-nine divisions on Warsaw

Pact M+15/NATO M+10. The Warsaw Pact would have a 2:1 advantage in armored division equivalents (ADEs) in the theater that would allow it to attain a local 6:1 advantage that might permit a major breakthrough so NATO prospects depended upon effective use of its reserves and timely arrival of US reinforcements. NATO might find it increasingly difficult to contain one breakthrough and still more difficult to contain more than one. The danger in the initial stages would be more acute if the Warsaw Pact accepted greater risks by reducing its forces in secondary sectors to attain an 8:1 advantage in ADEs in primary sectors.[19] The study also assessed an attack on a broad front at Warsaw Pact M+15 and with one hundred divisions at M+35. In both cases, Warsaw Pact forces could probably gain territory, perhaps to the line of the Weser and Lech rivers, and the outcome of the war would depend on the abilities of both sides to endure attrition and to sustain forces.[20]

There was also increased concern about US prospects in a war with the Soviet Union in the Persian Gulf in 1979. There had been an assumption in the 1970s that US forces assisting Iran would be making an "administrative" entry. Brown stated in 1979 that Soviet forces in the vicinity of the Persian Gulf could probably overwhelm Iranian forces so Iran might require US reinforcements, especially if the readiness of Soviet forces was raised, a process that might take several weeks.[21] This changed after the Iranian Revolution in February 1979, when the US would be making a forced entry into an Iran that was not necessarily friendly, and potentially in the face an invading Soviet force. The problem was even more severe after the Soviet intervention in Afghanistan in December 1979 because Soviet forces could attack from the east as well as the north and Soviet aircraft in Afghanistan could attack commercial shipping and military forces in the Persian Gulf. Brown was clear that the US had insufficient forces with which to confront a Soviet attack on Iran or elsewhere in the Persian Gulf, stating in February 1980 that "We can't assure you we could win a war there. . . . The commitment is to fight. It would be a mistake to assume a war between the United States and the Soviet Union can be won by either side."[22] Brown stated on February 15 that "the Soviet's couldn't count on" a confrontation with US forces remaining confined to the Persian Gulf region.[23] Given the size of forces the US could project into the region when the statement was made, Brown's assessment seems fair.

Carter signed PD-62 and PD-63 in January 1981 as a summing-up and a reference for the incoming Reagan administration. They articulated a shift of US resources from Europe and Asia to the Persian Gulf region because of the threat to the US, Europe, and Japan posed by Soviet activities and potential influence there. PD-62 *Modifications in U.S. National Security Strategy*, which modified PD-18, stated that Soviet activities in the Horn of Africa and its intervention in Afghanistan had substantially increased the threat to

US interests in the Persian Gulf, and the revolution in Iran, the war between Iran and Iraq, and the intensifying intra-Arab and Arab-Israeli tensions had increased the instability in the region and created opportunities for the Soviet Union while normalization of relations with China had improved the US situation in Asia.

> Given the danger that Soviet success in asserting influence over the oil producing status [sic] of the Persian Gulf region could undermine the viability of NATO and Japan, cause enormous economic disruptions in Europe, Japan, and the United States, higher priority must be given to developing adequate strategic lift, general purpose forces and facilities access for Persian Gulf contingencies.

While the US would continue to emphasize capability to defend Europe from Soviet attack, the Persian Gulf would have the highest priority for improvement of strategic lift and general purpose forces. The US would continue to improve relations with China and would call on Japan to increase its military capabilities.[24] PD-63 *Persian Gulf Security Framework* reiterated Carter's statement that "An attempt by any outside force to gain control of the Persian Gulf region will be regarded as an assault on the vital interests of the United States." The US would increase its ability to project forces into the region and would develop a range of military and non-military options in and beyond the region to compensate for the current Soviet regional advantage in conventional forces. US allies in Europe and Northeast Asia would be asked to carry more of the burden in their regions to offset the greater allocations of US resources to the Persian Gulf region.[25]

The Reagan administration was also concerned about the ability of the US to defend its interests. The first of two NSC meetings convened to discuss NSSD 1-82, the review of national strategy, focused on the Persian Gulf region. General Jones, the Chairman of the JCS, stated that a recent war game had shown "that we could hold in Iran for a while, but would eventually lose" even with optimistic assumptions. Secretary of Defense Caspar Weinberger stated "The threat of escalation is the key" and "The realities dictate that we cannot defend in place."[26] The second meeting discussed general purpose forces. On this issue, NSSD 1-82 was briefed as saying:

> ... in a conflict with the Soviet Union, we must undertake sequential operations and establish clear priorities ... In a conventional war with the Soviet Union, we ought to be able to deploy our forces rapidly to deter further aggression, attempt to halt the Soviet advances and prepare to execute counteroffensives where appropriate, with the words "where appropriate" being very important.

NSSD 1-82 was then quoted as saying "the US does not now possess a credible capability to achieve all military objectives simultaneously. In the midterm we will remain unable to meet the requirements for simultaneous global operations."[27]

The resulting NSDD-32 *U.S. National Security Strategy* stated that there had been "overwhelming growth of Soviet conventional forces capabilities." The Soviet Union was aware of the catastrophic consequences of initiating military action directly against the US or its allies so war was more likely to originate in regional tensions or a conflict with a Soviet client state. Though existing forces were likely sufficient to dissuade the Soviet Union from deliberate hostilities, the US required substantially more capable forces to have good prospects of defending its interests in case of war. NATO needed significantly improved general purpose forces. A key objective in Southwest Asia was to improve US ability to deploy and sustain forces to ensure that any Soviet attack would be confronted with the prospect of a major conflict with the US in the theater and the threat of escalation. The modernization of US strategic forces and "the achievement of parity with the Soviet Union" would receive first priority in US efforts to rebuild its military capabilities. Given current insufficiencies in general purpose forces, the US might not achieve some regional objectives, some commitments to some allies might not be honored, and the US might be forced to resort to nuclear weapons early in a conflict. The US would close the gap by improving the readiness, command and control, sustainability, mobility, and modernity of existing general purpose forces and then produce additional military capabilities. Nuclear forces would not be viewed as a lower-cost alternative but would remain an element in overall US strategy. The US would address its growing vulnerability to nuclear attack by enhancing the survivability of its strategic forces and improving continuity of government, command and control, and civil defense.[28]

CONCLUSIONS

The US leadership assessed US prospects in a war with the Soviet Union as worsening between the mid-1970s and the early 1980s. Where the Ford and Carter administrations had demonstrated some concern about the distribution of military capabilities and US prospects in a war with the Soviet Union in 1977 in Europe, the Carter administration in 1980 and 1981 and the Reagan administration in 1982 evinced considerable concern about US prospects in Europe and the Persian Gulf and the need for increased US military capabilities to improve them. This is consistent with the expectations of balance of military capabilities.

NOTES

1. NSSM 246 *National Defense Policy and Military Posture*, September 2, 1976. Box 2, National Security Decision Memoranda and Study Memoranda, Gerald R. Ford Library.
2. "National Security Council Meeting Minutes," December 15, 1976. Box 2, National Security Adviser. National Security Council Meetings File, Gerald R. Ford Library.
3. NSDM 348 *U.S. Defense Policy and Military Posture*, January 20, 1977. Box 1, National Security Decision Memoranda and Study Memoranda, Gerald R. Ford Library.
4. PRM/NSC-10 *Comprehensive Net Assessment and Military Posture Review*, Feb. 18, 1977 and Zbigniew Brzezinski, *Power and Principle: Memoirs of the National Security Adviser, 1977-1981* (New York: Farrar, Straus and Giroux, 1983), pp. 51–52.
5. Brzezinski, *Power and Principle*, p. 177.
6. PRM/NSC-10 *Military Strategy and Force Posture Review Final Report*, 1977, pp. 9–10.
7. Ibid., p. II-5.
8. PD/NSC-18 *U.S. National Strategy*, August 24, 1977, pp. 1–2.
9. Brzezinski, *Power and Principle*, p. 177. The relevant sections of PD/NSC-18 have been redacted.
10. Charles Mohr, "Carter Orders Steps to Increase Ability to Meet War Threats," *New York Times*, August 26, 1977, p. 1 and p. 42.
11. PD/NSC-18, pp. 3–5. See also PD/NSC-12 *U.S. Policy in Korea*, May 5, 1977.
12. *Report of Secretary of Defense Donald H. Rumsfeld to the Congress on the FY 1978 Budget, FY 1979 Authorization Request and FY 1978–1982 Defense Programs*, January 17, 1977 (hereafter *Report* (year)), p. 109.
13. "Statement by Harold Brown, February 22, 1977," *Survival* 23, no. 3 (May/June 1977), p. 122.
14. *Report* (1979), p. 16.
15. *Report* (1980), pp. 8–9.
16. Joint Chiefs of Staff, *United States Military Posture for FY 1981: A Supplement to the Chairman's Overview*, p. 24.
17. Ibid., p. 16.
18. Office of the Secretary of Defense/Program Analysis and Evaluation, *NATO Center Region Military Balance Study, 1978–1984*, July 13, 1979, p. I-29 and p. I-30.
19. Ibid., p. I-34.
20. Ibid., p. I-38 and p. I-39.
21. *Report* (1979), p. 107.
22. George C. Wilson, "Advocates of More Defense Spending Press Carter to Increase '81 Budget," *Washington Post*, February 1, 1980, p. A8.
23. Richard Halloran, "Brown Warns That a Persian Gulf War Could Spread," *New York Times*, February 15, 1980, p. 3.

24. PD/NSC-62 *Modifications in U.S. National Security Strategy*, January 15, 1981.
25. PD/NSC-63 *Persian Gulf Security Framework*, January 15, 1981.
26. "National Security Council Meeting," April 16, 1982, at Jason Salton-Ebin, "The Reagan Files," www.thereaganfiles.com.
27. "National Security Council Meeting," April 27, 1982, p. 3, ibid.
28. NSDD-32 *U.S. National Security Strategy*, May 20, 1982.

Chapter Seven

Conclusions

Balance of power and balance of threat provide competing, but related, explanations of balancing. They are related in that both expect countries to engage in balancing to maintain their independence. They differ in what causes balancing. According to balance of power, countries balance against power. Power is comprised of material resources like economic size, military expenditures, and number of military personnel. Balance of threat claims to refine and improve upon balance of power. In addition to power, it argues that balancing is caused by a country appearing especially dangerous because it has offensive power, geographic proximity, and aggressive intentions. Balance of threat allows a powerful country to balance against a weaker country and so to become stronger, something contrary to balance of power.

I argued in chapter 1 that there are gaps in the logics of balance of power and balance of threat, and I proposed a third explanation of balancing behavior, balance of military capabilities, to fill these gaps. Balance of military capabilities argues that countries balance against the ability of another country to conquer or compel them.

Chapter 1 articulated four observable implications that allow a test of balance of power, balance of threat, and balance of military capabilities and proposed the intensified US balancing against the Soviet Union in the early 1980s as a case with which to conduct the test. The first observable implication was about the distribution of power. Chapter 2 assessed the distribution of population, military personnel, and economic resources and chapter 3 assessed military expenditures. The second was whether the US perceived that the Soviet Union had aggressive intentions. Chapter 4 assessed US perceptions of Soviet intentions. The third was about the distribution of military capabilities. Chapter 5 assessed general purpose forces. The fourth was about

US assessments of its prospects in a war with the Soviet Union, which were evaluated in chapter 6.

The next section summarizes the evidence about these observable implications to assess which theory better explains US balancing behavior against the Soviet Union in the early 1980s.

OBSERVABLE IMPLICATIONS

Balance of Power

The first observable implication is about the distribution of power. In the bipolar distribution of power of the Cold War, both classical realist and neorealist balance of power theories expect that the US was concerned about the level and change of Soviet power. If balance of power is correct, the Soviet Union should be increasingly more powerful than the US. Balance of power would also be fortified if the Warsaw Pact was increasingly more powerful than the West. Balance of power will be infirmed if the US was more powerful than the Soviet Union or if the West was more powerful than the Warsaw Pact.

The US was more powerful than the Soviet Union and the West was more powerful than the Warsaw Pact. Chapter 2 showed the US economy was larger, more sophisticated, and growing faster than the Soviet economy. In terms of GNP, a measure of the aggregate size of an economy, US GNP was larger than Soviet GNP in terms of the latter's production possibility, and G-5 GNP was much larger than Warsaw Pact GNP. CIA measured production possibility rather than consumer welfare, and the difference between US and Soviet GNP was much larger if the latter was measured in terms of consumer welfare.

In terms of per capita GNP, an indicator of the sophistication of an economy, US per capita GNP was much higher than Soviet per capita GNP in terms of production possibility, and the difference was much greater in terms of consumer welfare. Regardless of how per capita GNP was measured, the smaller US population was much more productive than the Soviet population. This higher productivity indicates that the US had a more sophisticated economy than the Soviet Union, and further warrants that the US was more powerful in terms of economic elements of power than the Soviet Union.

The Soviet economy was growing slowly and had little prospect of increasing its growth rate over long periods of time; while the US economy was troubled, it had the possibility of faster future growth and higher long-term growth potential. CIA estimated in the mid-1970s that Soviet GNP was reaching the limits of extensive growth and was likely to encounter resource bottlenecks and so would grow between one and three percent in 1970 rubles depending on oil production. Others emphasized administrative inefficiency, the slow growth of factor productivity, and the burden of military expenditures. Importantly, the Soviet economy appeared to have little prospect for moving from extensive to intensive growth. With the exception of oil production, which was derivative of productivity, these factors reinforced each other to cause the Soviet economy to grow on average about two percent over the period 1981–1984 in 1982 rubles and 2.4 percent in 1970 rubles.

Differences between the US and Soviet economies were so great that precise values were not important. The Soviet economy was about half the size of the US economy when measured in rubles and about three-quarters the size when measured in its ability to produce the Soviet mix of output, marketable or not, in dollars. In either case, the difference in 1977 was some trillion 1976 rubles and a half trillion 1976 dollars. Inasmuch as the Soviet Union was unable to produce the US mix, the smaller, ruble, size was the relevant comparison. Similarly, the productivity difference between the US and Soviet populations was measured in thousands of 1976 rubles and dollars per person. If the smaller economy of the Soviet Union was confined to two percent real growth while the larger US economy had real growth of two to three percent, the differences in size and productivity would increase over time.

Second, it was clear that military expenditures imposed a heavy burden on the Soviet economy while the US burden was comparatively light. Contemporary CIA assessments, discussed in Chapter 3, estimated after 1976 that Soviet military expenditures were eleven to thirteen percent of GNP with expenditures increasing four to five per cent, much faster than GNP growth. Some contemporary estimates were much higher: Lee estimated fourteen to fifteen percent of GNP, while Marshall and Graham estimated up to twenty percent. In retrospect, it appears that, using CIA data, the Soviet burden was almost fifteen percent. Where what is striking about Soviet expenditures is the heaviness of the burden they imposed, what is striking about the US burden (and that of other Western countries) is its lightness: the US burden ranged from 4.6 percent in 1979 to a peak of 6.2 percent in 1986 and averaged 5.5 percent of GDP between 1977 and 1989.

Third, in terms of military expenditures in a common currency, CIA regularly estimated Soviet expenditures in dollars and occasionally calculated US expenditures in rubles. Use of a common currency allowed comparison of the size of the US and Soviet military programs. Dollar estimates estimated what it would cost the US to purchase the Soviet military program in the US as an alternate US program and so estimated the cost of producing, manning, and operating the Soviet military force using US costs and efficiencies. Soviet personnel, for example, were paid US rates, Soviet equipment designs were costed as if produced in the US with US manufacturing efficiencies and US profit margins, and these forces were costed as if operated using Soviet practices at US costs. Ruble estimates of US expenditures were calculations using ruble-dollar ratios and did not attempt to cost the US program as a Soviet alternative.

CIA estimated in 1979 that Soviet military expenditures in 1978 were 146 billion 1978 dollars when comparable US expenditures were $102 billion, estimated in 1978 that Soviet expenditures in 1977 were 130 billion 1977 dollars when comparable US expenditures were $90 billion, and estimated in 1977 that Soviet expenditures in 1976 were about 118 billion 1975 dollars when US defense outlays were $84 billion. CIA estimated in 1974 that US expenditures amounted to some 23.4 billion rubles, about 10 percent less than Soviet expenditures of 25.5 billion rubles.

Chapter 3 argues that CIA methodology for estimating Soviet expenditures in dollars, which populated the Soviet military with US personnel, did not estimate the cost of the Soviet program as an alternate program in which US personnel were treated and trained using Soviet practices and so probably overstated Soviet expenditures. I provided an alternate estimate in chapter 3 that Soviet expenditures in 1977 were some 82.2 to 84.1 billion 1977 dollars when US expenditures were $90 billion.

Hence, the US had a larger, more sophisticated economy than the Soviet Union, and the economies of the West were larger and more sophisticated than those of the Warsaw Pact. The US and the Soviet Union devoted similar levels of expenditures to military purposes, but Soviet expenditures imposed a much heavier burden on the Soviet economy. While Warsaw Pact military personnel slightly exceeded NATO personnel, the number of Warsaw Pact personnel was dwarfed by Chinese personnel. The Soviet Union was not more powerful than the US, and the Warsaw Pact was not more powerful than the West. Balance of power does not explain US balancing behavior and is infirmed.

Balance of Threat

Given that the US was more powerful than the Soviet Union, balance of threat has an opportunity to explain US balancing behavior. The crucial element of balance of threat is aggressive intentions. Balance of threat expects that a more powerful country will balance if it perceives that a weaker country has aggressive intentions, defined as a high propensity to attempt to compel it. Such compellence may involve initiation of war or, because a country may initiate hostilities in response to attempted compellence, acceptance of the risk that attempted compellence may lead to war. The observable implication is that the US perceived the Soviet Union as having a high propensity to attempt to compel the US and so might initiate hostilities or accept risks that might lead to war.

Analysis of National Intelligence Estimates between 1970 and 1982 shows that, beginning in 1976, the US intelligence community generally assessed the Soviet Union as desiring global hegemony but as unwilling to attempt to compel the US to attain it. Soviet intentions were not benign, but they were conditioned by the distribution of military capabilities and actualization of Soviet aspirations depended upon US decisions about how much military capability it would maintain. Analysis of US national security strategy statements between 1977 and 1982 and the views of the members of and advisers to the Ford, Carter, and Reagan NSCs show that there was not a dominant view that the Soviet Union had a high propensity to attempt to compel the US and so might initiate war or run risks that might lead to war. Hence, the US did not perceive the Soviet Union as having aggressive intentions and US balancing behavior is not explained by balance of threat.

Balance of Military Capabilities

Given that the US was more powerful than the Soviet Union and the West was more powerful than the Warsaw Pact so US balancing is not explained by balance of power, and the US did not perceive the Soviet Union as having aggressive intentions so US balancing is not explained by balance of threat, balance of military capabilities has an opportunity. Balance of military capabilities has two observable implications. The first is about the distribution of military capabilities. Balance of military capabilities explains US balancing by arguing that US military capabilities were not sufficient for it to be confident about its ability to defend vital territory and interests against a Soviet attack.

Chapter 5 assessed US and Soviet general purpose forces. It found that the US could have confidence in the ability of NATO to defend Europe only in the particular circumstances of a short-warning attack before the Warsaw Pact was fully mobilized or after US reinforcements were deployed in Europe. The US could not have high confidence in the ability of NATO to defend Europe in the case of an attack after the Warsaw Pact was largely mobilized but before US reinforcements deployed or if NATO mobilization lagged Warsaw Pact mobilization. Increasing Warsaw Pact capability meant the distribution of military capabilities would continue to move against the US unless the US and NATO increased their own capability. The US situation worsened in 1979 when the Iranian Revolution in February removed the regional US ally which would have provided a friendly reception to US forces in the Persian Gulf. The introduction of Soviet forces into Afghanistan in December apparently improved Soviet ability to introduce forces into the Persian Gulf region. The US was poorly positioned to defend its interests in the region and faced requirements for additional capability to have confidence that it could defend its interests. The increasing difficulties of defending Central Europe and the Persian Gulf argue in favor of a balance of military capabilities explanation.

The second observable implication is the perception of a country's leadership about its prospects in war. Balance of military capabilities explains US balancing by arguing that the US leadership was not confident that the US had good prospects in a war with the Soviet Union and generated military capability so that it would. Chapter 6 examined how the US leadership assessed US prospects in a war with the Soviet Union and concluded that US prospects were perceived as worsening between the mid-1970s and the early 1980s. Where the Ford and Carter administrations in 1977 had demonstrated some concern about the distribution of military capabilities and US prospects in a war with the Soviet Union in Europe, the Carter administration in 1980 and 1981 and the Reagan administration in 1982 evinced considerable concern about US prospects in Europe and elsewhere and the need for increased US military capability to improve them. This is consistent with the expectations of balance of military capabilities.

US military capability appeared increasingly insufficient over the late 1970s to provide a high confidence defense against a Soviet attack in Europe, US military capability appeared insufficient after 1979 to provide a high confidence defense of vital US interests in the Persian Gulf against a Soviet attack there, and US leaders did not have high confidence about US prospects in either of these theaters. This increasing insufficiency over time accords with the expectations of balance of military capabilities. At no time in the mid- to late 1970s did US leaders assess that US forces were sufficient for a high confidence defense of Europe, and US leaders did not assess that US forces were sufficient for a high confidence defense of the Persian Gulf after 1979. There is therefore a warrant for a balance of military capabilities explanation of US balancing.

BALANCE OF THREAT REVISITED

How might balance of threat respond? Balance of threat argues that the powerful US balanced against the weaker Soviet Union because the latter had offensive power and aggressive intentions. Balance of threat says that intentions are "crucial" and it is "cautious" about the significance of offensive power. I argue that the US did not perceive the Soviet Union to be particularly aggressive in this period so the crucial element of balance of threat is not present and the theory does not explain the case. Balance of threat might be conceptualized without its crucial component, aggressive intentions, and as emphasizing offensive power, about which it is cautious. However, to emphasize what it is cautious about and to deemphasize what it characterizes as crucial discounts the thrust of balance of threat.

Some might object that my definition of aggressive intentions sets the threshold too high. They might argue that assessments in the intelligence community that the Soviet Union aspired to global hegemony constitute perception that the Soviet Union had aggressive intentions. There are two objections. First, the countries Walt uses to illustrate aggressive intentions (Nazi Germany, Libya, and Wilhelmine Germany) attempted compellence and even initiated wars. They were not satisfied by aspiration, they ran risks and initiated hostilities. Second, they were comparatively insensitive to the distribution of military capabilities and yet engaged in offensive action. No one assessed the Soviet Union as insensitive to US military capabilities, and even Air Force intelligence and Team B in 1976 viewed the situation as one in which the US was allowing the Soviet Union to gain an advantage in military capability that the US could offset by increasing its own.

CONCLUSION

Of the two older theories, balance of threat is the challenger and so must yield to the established balance of power if their explanations are equally sound. As the challenger of established theories, balance of military capabilities should yield to the first two if either of them is sound and so should be tested third. Thus, the sequence to evaluate these theories was to consider balance of power, then balance of threat, and then balance of military capabilities. Balance of power would be fortified if the US was weaker than the Soviet Union or if the West was weaker than the Warsaw Pact. The US was more powerful than the Soviet Union and the West was more powerful than the Warsaw Pact so US behavior is not explained by balance of power. Balance of threat would be fortified if the US perceived that the Soviet Union had aggressive intentions. The absence of a dominant perception of aggressive intentions infirms balance of threat. Balance of military capabilities would be fortified if US military capabilities were insufficient to defend vital territories and interests from a Soviet attack and the US leadership was not confident that the US had good prospects in a war with the Soviet Union. The increasing insufficiency of US military capability and perceptions by US leaders that the US did not have good prospects in a war with the Soviet Union in the late 1970s means that increases in US military capability are readily explained by balance of military capabilities.

Bibliography

Allen, Thomas B. *War Games*. New York: McGraw-Hill, 1987.
Amman, Ronald, Julian Cooper, and R. W. Davies, eds. *The Technological Level of Soviet Industry*. New Haven: Yale University Press, 1977.
Aslund, Anders. "How Small is Soviet National Income?" In Rowen and Wolf, eds. *The Impoverished Superpower*.
Barron, John. *MiG Pilot: The Final Escape of Lieutenant Belenko*. New York: Reader's Digest, 1980.
Baxter, William P. *Soviet AirLand Battle Tactics*. Novato, CA: Presidio, 1986.
Becker, Abraham. "Intelligence Fiasco or Reasoned Accounting? CIA Estimates of Soviet GNP." *Post-Soviet Affairs* 10, no. 4 (1994).
——. "Revisiting Postwar Soviet Economic Performance." In Kennan Institute. *U.S. Assessments of the Soviet and Post-Soviet Russian Economy: Lessons Learned and Not Learned*. Washington: Woodrow Wilson Center, March 2002.
Berkowitz, Daniel M. et al. "Survey Article: An Evaluation of the CIA's Analysis of Soviet Economic Performance, 1970-1990." *Comparative Economic Studies* 35, no. 2 (Summer 1993).
Betts, Richard K. *Surprise Attack*. Washington, DC: Brookings, 1982.
Biddle, Stephen. *Military Power: Explaining Victory and Defeat in Modern Battle*. Princeton: Princeton University Press, 2004.
——. "Rebuilding the Foundations of Offense-Defense Theory." *Journal of Politics* 63, no. 3 (2001).
Brown, Harold. "Statement by Harold Brown, February 22, 1977." *Survival* 23, no. 3 (May/June 1977).
——. *Thinking About National Security: Defense and Foreign Policy in a Dangerous World*. Boulder, CO: Westview, 1983.
Brzezinski, Zbigniew. *Power and Principle: Memoirs of the National Security Adviser, 1977-1981*. New York: Farrar, Straus and Giroux, 1983.
Cahn, Anne Hessing. *Killing Détente: The Right Attacks the CIA*. University Park, PA: Pennsylvania State University Press, 1998.

Cahn, Anne Hessing and John Prados. "Team B: The Trillion Dollar Experiment." *Bulletin of the Atomic Scientists* 49, no. 3 (April 1993).
Carter, Jimmy. *Keeping Faith: Memoirs of a President*. New York: Bantam, 1982.
———. *Public Papers of the Presidents of the United States: Jimmy Carter, 1977*. Washington, DC: US GPO, 1977.
———. *Public Papers of the Presidents of the United States: Jimmy Carter, 1978*. Washington, DC: US GPO, 1978.
Jimmy Carter Library and Museum. Atlanta, GA. http://www.jimmycarterlibrary.gov/documents.
Castillo, Jasen, et al. *Military Expenditures and Economic Growth*. Santa Monica, CA: RAND, 2001.
Central Intelligence Agency. Freedom of Information Act Electronic Reading Room. http://www.foia.cia.gov.
Chirot, Daniel, ed. *The Crisis of Leninism and the Decline of the Left: The Revolutions of 1989*. Seattle: University of Washington Press, 1991.
Claude, Jr., Inis L. *Power and International Relations*. New York: Random House, 1962.
Cockle, Paul. "Analysing Soviet Defense Spending: the Debate in Perspective." *Survival* 20, no. 5 (September/October 1978).
Collins, John M. *American and Soviet Military Trends Since the Cuban Missile Crisis*. Washington, DC: Center for Strategic and International Studies, 1978.
Collins, John M. and Anthony H. Cordesman. *Imbalance of Power: Shifting U.S.-Soviet Military Strengths*. San Rafael, CA: Presidio, 1978.
Congressional Budget Office. *U.S. Airlift Forces: Enhancement Alternatives for NATO and Non-NATO Contingencies*. Washington, DC: US GPO, 1979.
Correlates of War. http://www.correlatesofwar.org.
Donnelly, Christopher. *Red Banner: The Soviet Military System in Peace and War*. Coulsdon, Surrey: Jane's Information Group, 1988.
———. "The Soviet Soldier: Behavior, Performance, Effectiveness." In John Erickson and E. J. Feuchtwanger, eds. *Soviet Military Power and Performance*. Hamden, CT: Archon, 1979.
Easterly, William and Stanley Fischer. "The Soviet Economic Decline." *World Bank Economic Review* 9, no. 3 (September 1995).
Eberstadt, Nicholas. *The Tyranny of Numbers: Mismeasurement and Misrule*. Washington, DC: American Enterprise Institute, 1995.
Edwards, Imogene, Margaret Hughes, and James Noren. "US and USSR: Comparisons of GNP." In Joint Economic Committee. *Soviet Economy in a Time of Change*. Washington, DC: US GPO, 1979.
Epstein, David F. "The Economic Cost of Soviet Security and Empire." In Rowen and Wolf, eds. *The Impoverished Superpower*.
Evera, Stephen Van. *Causes of War: Power and the Roots of Conflict*. Ithaca: Cornell University Press, 1999.
Firth, Noel E. and James H. Noren. *Soviet Defense Spending: A History of CIA Estimates, 1950-1990*. College Station, TX: Texas A&M University Press, 1998.

Fischer, Robert Lucas. *Defending the Central Front: The Balance of Forces*. London: International Institute for Strategic Studies, 1976.
Gerald R. Ford Library. Ann Arbor, MI. http://www.fordlibrarymuseum.gov/library/docs.asp.
———. National Security Adviser. NSC Program Analysis Staff Files, Box 2, Defense Review Panel Meeting, November 24, 1976.
Ford, Harold P. *Estimative Intelligence: The Purposes and Problems of National Intelligence Estimating, Revised Edition*. Lanham, MD: University Press of America, 1993.
Gabriel, Richard A. *The Antagonists: A Comparative Combat Assessment of the Soviet and American Soldier*. Westport, CT: Greenwood, 1984.
Gaddis, John Lewis. *Strategies of Containment*. New York: Oxford University Press, 1982.
Garthoff, Raymond L. *Détente and Confrontation: American-Soviet Relations from Nixon to Reagan, Revised Edition*. Washington, DC: Brookings, 1994.
———. *The Great Transition: American-Soviet Relations and the End of the Cold War*. Washington, DC: Brookings, 1994.
Gates, Robert M. *From the Shadows: The Ultimate Insider's Story of Five Presidents and How They Won the Cold War*. New York: Simon & Schuster, 1996.
Glantz, David M. *Soviet Military Operational Art: In Pursuit of Deep Battle*. London: Frank Cass, 1991.
Government Accounting Office. *Soviet Economy: Assessment of How Well the CIA Has Estimated the Size of the Economy*. Washington, DC: 1991.
Graham, Daniel O. "The Soviet Military Budget Controversy." *Air Force*, May 1976.
Gulick, Edward Vose. *Europe's Classical Balance of Power*. New York: Norton, 1955.
Guttridge, Leonard F. *Mutiny: A History of Naval Insurrection*. Annapolis, MD: Naval Institute Press, 1992.
Herspring, Dale R. and Ivan Volgyes. "How Reliable are Eastern European Armies." *Survival* 22, no. 5 (September/October 1980).
Heston, Alan, Robert Summers and Bettina Aten. Penn World Table. Philadelphia: Center for International Comparisons of Production, Income and Prices at the University of Pennsylvania. http://www.pwt.econ.upenn.edu/php_site/pwt_index.php.
Hines, John G., Ellis M. Mishulovich, and John Shull. *Soviet Intentions 1965-1985. Volume I: An Analytical Comparison of U.S.-Soviet Assessments During the Cold War*. McLean, VA: BDM, September 22, 1995.
Holloway, David. *The Soviet Union and the Arms Race*. New Haven: Yale University Press, 1983.
Holzman, Franklyn D. "Politics and Guesswork: CIA and DIA Estimates of Soviet Military Spending." *International Security* 14, no. 2 (Fall 1989).
International Institute for Strategic Studies. *The Military Balance, 1979-1980*. London: International Institute for Strategic Studies, 1979.
———. *The Military Balance 1980-81*. New York: Facts on File, 1980.
Isby, David C. *Weapons and Tactics of the Soviet Army, Fully Revised Edition*. New York: Jane's, 1988.

Jervis, Robert. "Cooperation Under the Security Dilemma." *World Politics* 30, no. 2 (1978).

———. *System Effects: Complexity in Political and Social Life*. Princeton: Princeton University Press, 1997.

Joint Chiefs of Staff. *United States Military Posture for FY 1981: A Supplement to the Chairman's Overview*. Washington, DC, 1980.

Johnson, A. Ross, Robert W. Dean, and Alexander Alexiev. "The Armies of the Warsaw Pact Northern Tier." *Survival* 23, no. 4 (July/August 1981).

Kaufman, Robert G. "To Balance or to Bandwagon? Alignment Decisions in 1930s Europe." *Security Studies* 1, no. 3 (1992).

Kennedy, David M. *Sunshine and Shadow: The CIA and the Soviet Economy*. Harvard University Kennedy School of Government Case C16-91-1096.0 (1991).

Kissinger, Henry. *Years of Renewal*. New York: Simon & Schuster, 1999.

Kurtzweg, Laurie Rogers. *Measures of Soviet Gross National Product in 1982 Prices: A Study Prepared for the Joint Economic Committee of the United States Congress*. Washington, DC: US GPO, 1990.

Lee, William T. *CIA Estimates of Soviet Military Expenditures: Errors and Waste*. Washington, DC: American Enterprise Institute, 1995.

———. *The Estimation of Soviet Defense Expenditures, 1955-75: An Unconventional Approach*. New York: Praeger, 1977.

Levy, Jack S. "Balances and Balancing: Concepts, Propositions and Research Design," in Vasquez and Elman, eds., *Realism and the Balancing of Power*.

———. "What Do Great Powers Balance and When?" In *Balance of Power: Theory and Practice in the 21st Century*, edited by T.V. Paul, James J. Wirtz, and Michael Fortman. Stanford, CA: Stanford University Press, 2004.

MacEachin, Douglas. *Predicting the Soviet Invasion of Afghanistan: The Intelligence Community's Record*. Washington, DC: CIA, 2002.

———. *CIA Assessments of the Soviet Union: The Record Versus the Charges*. Washington, DC: CIA, 1996.

Marshall, Andrew. "Holding the Bridge." *National Interest* 62 (Winter 2000/01).

———. "Sources of Soviet Power: The Military Potential in the 1980s." In International Institute for Strategic Studies. *Prospects of Soviet Power in the 1980s, Part II*. London: International Institute for Strategic Studies, 1979.

Mastny, Vojtech and Malcolm Byrne. *A Cardboard Castle? An Inside History of the Warsaw Pact, 1955-1991*. New York: Central European University Press, 2005.

Mearsheimer, John J. *The Tragedy of Great Power Politics*. New York: Norton, 2001.

Meyer, Stephen M. *Soviet Theatre Nuclear Forces, Part I: Development of Doctrine and Objectives*. London: International Institute for Strategic Studies, 1983/1984.

———. *Soviet Theatre Nuclear Forces, Part II: Capabilities and Implications*. London: International Institute for Strategic Studies, 1983/1984.

Morgenthau, Hans J. *Politics Among Nations: The Struggle for Power and Peace, 5th ed*. New York: Knopf, 1978.

Moynihan, Brian. *Claws of the Bear: The History of the Red Army From the Revolution to the Present*. New York: Houghton Mifflin, 1989.

National Archives and Records Administration. College Park, MD. RG 263.

National Security Archive. Documents assembled for the symposium at Lysebu. Washington DC: 1995.
Odom, William E. *The Collapse of the Soviet Military*. New Haven: Yale University Press, 1998.
Office of Management and Budget. *The Budget for Fiscal Year 2001*. Washington, DC: US GPO, 2000.
Office of the Secretary of Defense/Program Analysis and Evaluation. *NATO Center Region Balance Study, 1978-1984*. Washington, DC: July 13, 1979.
Office of Technology Assessment. *New Technology for NATO: Implementing Follow-On Forces Attack*. Washington, DC: US GPO, 1987.
Pedlow, Gregory W. ed. *NATO Strategy Documents, 1949-1969*. http://www.nato.int/archives/strategy.htm.
Pipes, Richard. "Team B: The Reality Behind the Myth." *Commentary*, October 1986.
Polmar, Norman. *The Naval Institute Guide to the Soviet Navy, 5th Edition*. Annapolis: Naval Institute Press, 1986.
Prados, John. *The Soviet Estimate: U.S. Intelligence Analysis and Russian Military Strength*. New York: Dial, 1982.
Quester, George H. *Offense and Defense in the International System*. New York: Wiley, 1977.
Reese, Roger R. *The Soviet Military Experience*. New York: Routledge, 2000.
Rosen, Stephen Peter. *Winning the Next War: Innovation and the Modern Military*. Ithaca: Cornell University Press, 1991.
Rowen, Henry S. and Charles Wolf, Jr., eds. *The Impoverished Superpower: Perestroika and the Soviet Military Burden*. San Francisco: Institute for Contemporary Studies, 1990.
Salton-Ebin, Jason. "The Reagan Files." http://www.thereaganfiles.com.
Scherer, John L. *USSR Facts and Figures Annual 3, 1979*. Gulf Breeze, FL: Academic International Press, 1979.
Schroeder, Gertrude E. "Reflections on Economic Sovietology." *Post-Soviet Affairs* 11, no. 3 (1995).
Schweller, Randall. "Bandwagoning for Profit: Bringing the Revisionist State Back In." *International Security* 19, no. 1 (Summer 1994).
US Army. *FM 100-2-1 The Soviet Army: Operations and Tactics*. July 16, 1984.
US Congress. Senate Armed Services Committee. *NATO and the New Soviet Threat: Report of Sen. Sam Nunn and Sen. Dewey F. Bartlett*. Washington, DC: US GPO, 1977.
US Congress. *Congressional Record*. 95th Congress, 1st Session, 1977.
———. Joint Economic Committee. *Allocation of Resources in the Soviet Union and China — 1975*. 94th Congress, First Session, June 18 and July 21, 1975.
———. Joint Economic Committee. *Allocation of Resources in the Soviet Union and China — 1976*. 94th Congress, Second Session, May 24 and June 15, 1976.
———. Joint Economic Committee. *Allocation of Resources in the Soviet Union and China — 1977*. 95th Congress, First Session, June 23, 1977.
———. Joint Economic Committee. *Allocation of Resources in the Soviet Union and China — 1978*. 95th Congress, Second Session, June 26 and July 14, 1978.

———. Joint Economic Committee. *Allocation of Resources in the Soviet Union and China—1979*. 96th Congress, First Session, June 26 1979.

———. Senate Select Committee on Intelligence. *The National Intelligence Estimates A-B Team Episode Concerning Soviet Strategic Capability and Objectives*. 95th Congress, 2nd Session, 1978.

———. *The Soviet Oil Situation: An Evaluation of CIA Analyses of Soviet Oil Production*. Washington, DC: US GPO, 1978.

US Department of Commerce Bureau of Economic Analysis. *National Income and Product Accounts*. http://www.bea.gov/national/nipaweb/index.asp.

US Department of Defense. *Department of Defense Annual Report*.

———. *United States Military Posture for FY 1980: An Overview by Gen. David C. Jones, Chairman of the Joint Chiefs of Staff*. Washington, DC: 1979.

Vance, Cyrus. *Hard Choices: Critical Years in America's Foreign Policy*. New York: Simon & Schuster, 1983.

Vasquez, John A. and Colin Elman, eds. *Realism and the Balancing of Power: A New Debate*. Upper Saddle River, NJ: Prentice Hall, 2003.

Walt, Stephen M. "Alliance Formation and the Balance of World Power." *International Security* 9, no. 4 (Spring 1995).

———. "Containing Rogues and Renegades: Coalition Strategies and Counterproliferation." In *The Coming Crisis: Nuclear Proliferation, U.S. Interests, and World Order*, edited by Victor Utgoff. Cambridge, MA: MIT Press, 2000.

———. *The Origins of Alliances*. Ithaca: Cornell University Press, 1987.

———. "The Progressive Power of Realism." In *Realism and the Balancing of Power*, edited by Vasquez and Elman.

———. *Revolution and War*. Ithaca: Cornell University Press, 1996.

———. "Testing Theories of Alliance Formation: The Case of Southwest Asia." *International Organization* 42, no. 2 (Spring 1988).

Waltz, Kenneth N. "The Emerging Structure of International Politics." *International Security* 18, no. 2 (Fall 1993).

———. *Theory of International Politics*. New York: McGraw-Hill, 1979.

Wardak, Ghulam Dastagir. *The Voroshilov Lectures: Materials from the Soviet General Staff Academy, Volume I: Issues of Military Strategy*. Edited by Graham Hall Turbiville, Jr. Washington, DC: National Defense University Press, 1989.

Weinberger, Caspar. *Fighting for Peace: Seven Critical Years in the Pentagon*. New York: Warner, 1990.

Westerfield, H. Bradford, ed. *Inside CIA's Private World: Declassified Articles From the Agency's Internal Journal, 1955-1992*. New Haven: Yale University Press, 1995.

Wohlforth, William Curti. *The Elusive Balance: Power and Perceptions During the Cold War*. Ithaca: Cornell University Press, 1993.

Wolfers, Arnold. *Discord and Collaboration: Essays on International Politics*. Baltimore: Johns Hopkins University Press, 1962.

Zaloga, Steven J. *Red Thrust: Attack on the Central Front, Soviet Tactics and Capabilities in the 1990s*. Novato, CA: Presidio, 1989.

Index

Allen, Richard, 74

Belenko, Viktor, 41
Brezhnev, Leonid, 58, 59
Brown, Harold, 62, 64, 68, 69, 72, 98, 101-2, 103
Brzezinski, Zbigniew, 61, 64, 66, 67-68, 74, 77
Bush, George H. W., 24

Casey, William, 73, 74
Carter, Jimmy, 62-63, 64, 67, 68, 69, 72, 74, 77, 103, 104
Clark, William, 74
Claude, Inis, Jr., 6

Evera, Stephen Van, 10

Ford, Gerald, 58-59

Gaddis, John Lewis, 63
Garthoff, Raymond, 63, 69
Gates, Robert, 37, 38, 45, 62
Graham, Daniel, 36, 45, 110
Gulick, Edward Vose, 6-7

Haig, Alexander, 74
Huntington, Samuel, 99

index number problem, 20-21, 43-44

Jervis, Robert, 6, 10
Jones, David, 62, 63, 72, 104

Kissinger, Henry, 58, 63, 74

Lee, William, 36, 37, 45, 110
Levy, Jack, 6

MacEachin, Douglas, 26
Marshall, Andrew, 36, 37, 38, 45, 110
Mearsheimer, John, 7-8
military expenditures, narrow and broad definitions, 34, 38; methods of estimation, 32-33
Morgenthau, Hans, 6

neorealism, 7
NIE 11-3/8-76, 55-56, 59
NSDD-32, 75, 78, 105
NSDD-75, 75-76
NSDM-348, 59, 64, 99, 101
NSSD 1-82, 77, 104-5
NSSM-246, 59, 98, 101

Odom, William, 42

PD-18, 63-64, 100, 101
PD-62, 72-73, 103-4
PD-63, 72-73, 103-4
PFIAB, 55
Pipes, Richard, 76
power, 8
PRM-10, 98-100, 101

Quester, George, 10

Reagan, Ronald, 74
realism, classical, 6-7
Rumsfeld, Donald, 101

Schweitzer, Robert, 75-75
Solow-Denison model, 18

Team B, 55-58
Tighe, Eugene, 42
Turner, Stansfield, 24, 66, 70-72

Vance, Cyrus, 61-64, 67, 77

Walt, Stephen, 8-10, 114
Waltz, Kenneth, 6, 7
Weinberger, Caspar, 74, 104
Wolfers, Arnold, 6
Wohlforth, William, 6

www.ingramcontent.com/pod-product-compliance
Lightning Source LLC
Chambersburg PA
CBHW022016300426
44117CB00005B/211